Published by
NIYOGI BOOKS
D-78, Okhla Industrial Area, Phase-I
New Delhi-110 020, INDIA
Tel: 91-11-26816301, 49327000
Fax: 91-11-26810483, 26813830
email: niyogibooks@gmail.com
website: www.niyogibooksindia.com

Editor: Jayalakshmi Sengupta
Design: Ganga Kumar

ISBN: 978-93-85285-40-0
Publication: 2016

Printed at: Niyogi Offset Pvt. Ltd., New Delhi, India

Don't limit a child to your own learning, for he was born in another time.

—Rabindranath Tagore

Contents

Preface

As a professional physicist, I have worked in various colleges, institutions and universities, both in India and abroad. After a span of more than thirty-five years of service in different places in India, I came to Visva-Bharati (V-B), a truly unique university set up by Rabindranath Tagore. This experience, over the last four years or so, opened my eyes to aspects of education which, in its holistic and all-encompassing form, led me to think deeply about the meaning of education itself. These thoughts were reinforced by just the previous experience of leading a new experiment of integrated science education in India as the founding director of one of the two Indian Institutes of Science Education and Research that were set up in the year 2006. It is with this background that I embarked on the task of writing this monograph, which portrays in a positive manner the values and ideals that were enshrined in the mind of India's greatest thinker, Gurudev Tagore, more than one hundred and fifteen years ago. At the same time the book also contains a chapter on a critical analysis of how these values are getting increasingly eroded in the present rush for career oriented and straight jacketed education.

The monograph is a reflection on various Tagore–related topics, some of which are re-written versions of lectures I have given in different forums, including V-B, or translations from Bengali writings that had been co-authored with Dr Indrani Mukhopadhyay. I am much indebted to her and Dr N. Mukunda and Dr Sitansu Roy for their invaluable advice and suggestions.

This book starts with a personal account of where I see myself vis-à-vis Rabindranath Tagore today, especially after my appointment in this elite institution as its Vice Chancellor in the year (2011) when I experienced a tremendous transformation within me. It goes on to describe how I feel about Tagore's Visva-Bharati after a long stint in scientific institutions and science departments of universities. My other reflections include an analysis of Tagore as an institution-builder, a hitherto less-discussed topic that raises the important question of how contextual the values embedded in the founding father's vision are—especially today when many of the material objects and practices, prevalent in Tagore's days, have disappeared from our lives altogether. Since Rabindranath's views on education were anchored on Upanishadic thoughts that hinged on the interaction of man and nature, the difficult issue of how to interface a contemporary university with an idea and an ideal, fast disappearing under the onslaught of modern times, has also been explored.

This book also focuses on Tagore's Magnum Opus—*Gitanjali: Song Offerings* that fetched him Asia's first Nobel Prize. Several poems of *Gitanjali*, translated into English by Tagore himself, appear in *Song Offerings* and are sung in the form of 'Rabindrasangeet'. This book chronicles some of those songs, which were composed and published elsewhere, but which can be interpreted to reflect the seasonal changes of Birbhum. The effort to translate *Gitanjali* was not a premeditated attempt to cater to the English audience but a spontaneous wish to reach out to a wider readership. It is no wonder then that *Gitanjali* had since been translated into many non-English languages and the Nobel Prize to Tagore had instilled an Asian identity and self-belief.

It is well-known that Rabindranath was acutely uncomfortable with nationalistic sentiments, articulated by Gandhiji and his followers. Tagore's concept of humanity transcended national boundaries and into domains that are not restricted by country-specific priorities. Inevitably, numerous national and international personalities were drawn towards Tagore, who had occasions to interact with them on a range of issues: Indian identity, the freedom movement, education, East-West confluence, art and music. A limited sample of these famous encounters finds places in this book, too.

Rabindranath was primarily a poet and a philosopher, yet he had abiding interest in science from childhood. A tangibly powerful expression of that interest is the book called *Visva Parichay* (*An introduction to the Universe*) that he penned during the years 1934–37. Indeed, much of his focus on Visva-Bharati in the post-1920 years was on agricultural sciences, application of statistics, co-operative and mechanised farming, etc. Tagore perceived science not as a distinct intellectual pursuit from philosophy but as a unified holistic approach to unravel the beauty of creation. Inevitably, most of his creative thoughts on science are reflected in his music and shaped by his proximity to great scientists like Jagadish Chandra Bose—a close personal friend—and Albert Einstein. These aspects, namely the intersection of Rabindrasangeet with science, and a critical analysis of Tagore's meetings with Einstein, which have not been discussed earlier, are included in this book, hopefully without any prejudice.

Introduction

I grew up in a family not overly or overtly religious. My father, though not an atheist, hardly ever visited a temple. Worshipping, for him, was a private matter. So much so that he was opposed to the socio-religious event of Durga Puja, the biggest among the Bengalis, where the whole community got involved in this fanfare. He was equally against the growing cult of following religious gurus, babas, maharajas and swamis, who, he felt, often misled people and misused vulnerability in the name of religion. My mother, too, educated beyond the norm of the day while being deeply entrenched in the philosophy of Ramakrishna Paramahansa, remained equally averse to religiosity. In my youth I was further exposed to a turbulently questioning Bengal, torn by refugee influxes across its border, and steeped into progressive thinking that eventually led to a full-blown communist movement. As the years went by, my natural inclination led me to dedicate myself to the cause of scientific research, with no time for spirituality at all. After returning to India following a doctoral and two post-doctoral stints in North America for nearly seven years, I got intensely involved with teaching physics, researching and institution-building. My motto in life became: 'Work is Worship'.

It was against in this backdrop that, at the ripe age of nearly sixty-four, I entered the portals of a heritage university of India, called Visva-Bharati, as its Chief Executive or Vice Chancellor. This university, located

Open-air classes in Brahmacharya Ashram

in Santiniketan ('Abode of Peace'), 160 km north-west of Kolkata, was founded by the poet, philosopher and writer, Rabindranath Tagore, who went on to win Asia's first Nobel Prize in the year 1913.

Shortly after moving to Santiniketan in the year 1901, Tagore lost his wife and two children and resorted to living life of an ascetic in deep reflection. By then he had reached the midpoint of his life. He had turned spiritual, and had initiated a unique model of education that incorporated open-air classes through which he could help young children imbibe rudimentary scientific ideas as well as singing, dancing, painting and sculpting. The idea was to create an environment of holistic learning—an all-encompassing education combining Eastern Upanishadic thoughts with Western scientific temperament.

My exposure to Tagore had hitherto been limited to occasional indulgences in singing and listening to Rabindrasangeet—songs written and composed by Tagore. I had rarely delved into the lyrics or strived to comprehend the deep underlying meaning of the words when I was young. But gradually it dawned on me how every written word—be it on love, nature, history, science or philosophy—was infused with deep introspection.

Tagore had several admirers whom he deeply liked and loved, and drew creative inspiration from, so the term 'love' appeared strongly in all Tagore's works, throughout his life. One interesting musing on this subject, narrated in 'Paschim Yatri-r Diary', aboard the ship 'Krakovia', on 13 February 1925, translated from Bengali, reads:

> There are two words in Bengali to express 'prem'—emotional bonding: 'bhalolaga'—Self-driven adoration and 'bhalobasa'—Love. These two words symbolise two posts across the sea of emotion. When ego is involved, the expressive phrase is 'bhalolaga', but when others are involved, it is 'bhalobasa'. In adoration there is self-satiation, whereas in loving there is self-sacrifice.

The 'baul' songs of the Poet were an extension of this expression into mysticism, Sufi philosophy and detached love. It was a fascinating experience for me to find pieces of Rabindrasangeet that fitted to every mood and nuance of my existence. I was transfixed to the universal love that Tagore's songs exuded.

The other startling revelation was the connection between science, creation and Rabindrasangeet. It was apparent that the Bard was in tune with Quantum Theory, which addresses the notion of 'reality' in both its particle and wave senses. Tagore had even asked the great physicist Einstein: 'How do you know that the Moon is beautiful unless *you* observe it?', thus underscoring the omnipresence of the 'Observer' in what is being 'Observed'—an essential aspect of quantum mechanics. The concept of symmetry and symmetry-breaking, ensconced in the recently discovered Higgs Boson (popularly called the God Particle), is also a recurring theme in Tagore's songs. Tagore viewed life and death as two complementary phenomena located diametrically opposite on a cosmic wheel, just like day and night, happiness and grief, white and black, and so on. For me, personally, it was an entirely new way of visualising my own being.

Was Tagore religious? Not at all in the ritualistic sense; he saw imprints of the Creator in the splendour of nature—in the cosmos, trees, fields, animals, and above all, in human beings. When you participate in the weekly Wednesday prayers or in the slew of events like 'Briksharopan' (Tree-planting), 'Halakarshan' (Ploughing), 'Shilpotsav' (Craft Festival), 'Basantotsav' (Spring Festival), which take place at V-B, you experience contact with the Creator through the worship of Nature.

Today, I find myself standing at the crossroads of Science and Theology. While as a scientist I find explanations for the way every limb of the human body functions, and how the heart is a nonlinear electro-mechanical system that sends signals to the brain and regulates the viscosity of blood flow through arteries, I have no understanding of how the mind works. Are mind, emotion, and love not like quantum objects that can co-exist in simultaneous 'superposed' states that are 'entangled'?

Tagore's metaphor of a flower comes to mind. The existence of a flower, from the time a seed is planted, its nourishment through the soil, growth of the plant, formation of the bud…to its eventual blossoming, is a scientific phenomenon. But the perception of the flower and an appreciation of its beauty, based on its colour, shape, size, fragrance, is entirely in our mind, for which science does not seem to have a clue. This inexplicable connection with the Creator understood and explained through Rabindrasangeet has caused a remarkable transformation in my life. Tagore, through his songs, has become my messenger of this universal love, my counsellor, and my healer.

Gurudev's Views on Education

Santiniketan Griha

Visva-Bharati

Visva-Bharati (V-B), where the 'World makes its home in a single nest', is the brainchild of Rabindranath Tagore, but his name is not associated with it (by his own volition). This is unlike, say, Jawaharlal Nehru University (JNU), a public central university that was not founded by Jawaharlal Nehru. In fact, there are only a few universities in this world, like the Lubumba University of Moscow or the Humbold University of Berlin, that have individual's names attached to them. Therefore, there are deep reasons behind Tagore's christening his university Visva-Bharati. Each institute of V-B and its associated academic program has emanated from Tagore's emancipated mind, far-sighted concepts and creative thoughts, which are the subject-matter of the present discussion. The purpose of this section is to present the *unique* aspects of the university called Visva-Bharati, founded by India's Nobel Laureate poet, writer and philosopher, Rabindranath Tagore.

My experience of working in India, first in Presidency College, Kolkata, during 1968–69, and then a plethora of institutions: The Reactor Research Centre, Kalpakkam (1976–81), The Central University of Hyderabad (1981–86), JNU, New Delhi (1986–99), S.N. Bose National Centre for Basic Sciences (1999–2006), and the Indian Institute of Science Education & Research (2006–2011)—following a gap of seven years of doctoral and post-doctoral experience in North America—has all been in science-related

Above: *Basantotsav*
Below: *Briksharopan*

fields. With this background the arrival in Visva-Bharati in September of 2011 was an eye-opener.

Tagore established an 'Ashram-Vidyalaya' in Santiniketan in 1901, for the following reasons, I think: First, there was a need to be away from the capital city of Kolkata and the concomitant colonial influence on education; second, the seasonal variety of Santiniketan had an abiding appeal to the Poet, who viewed nature as a living laboratory; third, the young Robi had felt 'caged' during his not-too-long school experience, and hence wanted to introduce a system of classes held under the trees wherein children could be exposed to seasonal changes, photo-synthesis, basic entomology, not to mention music and dance. Finally, the presence of 'bauls' in Santiniketan and their aligning philosophy with Sufis had a great attraction for Tagore. It is from these motivating factors that emerged today's Ananda and Santosh Pathshalas, as well as Patha-Bhavana and Siksha-Satra. The Ananda Pathshala is a pre-school to Patha-Bhavana, located in Santiniketan whereas Santosh Pathshala, a similar pre-school to Siksha-Satra, is situated about five kilometres away in Sriniketan.

The present educational scenario of the world sees a lot of emphasis on school education that provides the right platform for learning such subjects as mathematics and languages. Therefore, Tagore's idea of organically bonding basic education with research under the unitary umbrella of the same university was a unique concept indeed.

Two schools of music and fine arts started in tandem in 1919. Tagore had used these two creative attributes as the medium for his motto in life—philosophy, spirituality, history, geography, science, environment-studies, and so on. If we can unify Kala-Bhavana (in Santiniketan) with Shilpo-Sadana (in adjoining Sriniketan) we can nucleate a modern institute of design that has no parallel in Indian universities. Tagore's songs were an assimilation of Hindustani classical music and Western music, and his dance forms had imbibed Manipuri, Kathakali and Candy styles, yielding something akin to a chemical reaction wherein the reacting agents lose their identity, just as we cannot decipher the separate presences of sodium and chlorine in common salt.

The next unique component of V-B is the Sriniketan experiment of agriculture, community teaching and 'rural reconstruction'. When combined with our School of Education (Vinaya-Bhavana) and science programs of Botany, Zoology and Biotechnology, these Sriniketan activities can go a long way in making V-B a model university. In addition, the various festivities of 'Briksharopan' (Tree-planting), 'Halakarshan' (Ploughing), and 'Basantotsav' (Spring Festival) provide a backdrop to Tagore's concern for the environment, which, in today's context of climate issues, assumes a significant dimension for modern education.

Finally, one must mention the Poet's deep moorings into Vedantic and Upanishadic thoughts and their juxtaposition with Buddhist philosophy. That is why he had invited Chinese, Japanese and other Buddhist scholars to Santiniketan to initiate Cheena-Bhavana, Nippon-Bhavana, Indo-Tibetan studies and Buddhist studies in order to provide a forum for East-West harmony.

To return to the point where I started, it can be seen how a large university came into being, brick by brick with the multidimensional ideas of a far-sighted, sensitive and creative genius. Unfortunately, today we seem to have deviated substantially from the great ideals of holistic education by creating partitions amongst disciplines. The time has come to remind ourselves of the immortal lines from *Gitanjali* to remember what a university should be like:

> Where the mind is without fear and the head is held high;
> Where knowledge is free;
> Where the world has not been broken up into fragments by
> narrow domestic walls;
> Where words come out from the depth of truth;
> Where tireless striving stretches its arms towards perfection;
> Where the clear stream of reason has not lost its way into the
> dreary desert sand of dead habit;
> Where the mind is led forward by Thee into ever-widening
> thought and action—

Tagore—the Educationist and Institution Builder

Tagore was not just a Nobel Laureate but an extraordinary institution-builder and a visionary educationist; a man whose thoughts transcended international boundaries and time zones; and above all, a universalist who viewed education as a holistic, all-encompassing human endeavour, unifying arts and sciences.

Tagore's deep love for nature, his eternal fascination for the marvel of creation and the energy his songs exude, is often in sharp contrast to Tagore's paintings, which portray a sense of sadness and melancholy. His songs as well as his ideas of comprehensive education, including scientific enquiry, carry the message of vitality or vibration, what the Poet called 'spandan', 'taranga'. Be it outdoor classes, exploration of nature, rural reconstruction, or his passionate attraction to the deductive logic of science—the Poet extols the power of vibration.

Visva-Bharati is an epitome of borderless education where 'Visva' is the World or, more generally, the Universe—hence the connotation of a 'University'! A university, according to Tagore, did not belong to Santiniketan or Birbhum or West Bengal or India but to the entire world. Here people, faculty and students, should come from all over the world, stay in its campus, interact and carry out teaching and research. Tagore believed in our traditions, which are deeply rooted in the Eastern civilisation of India, Persia, China and Japan. But he also wanted an assimilation of Western thoughts and ideals.

Above: *Rabindranath Tagore with Mahatma Gandhi*
Below: *Jawaharlal Nehru with Rabindranath Tagore*

The word 'Bharati' is a remarkable phrase with multiple meanings. 'Bharati' is Saraswati, Goddess of Learning, yet 'Bharati' also denotes 'Bharat', India, and 'Visva-Bharati' is therefore a seat of learning in India, but open to the whole world. It is a place where East meets West, to unravel the beauty and truth of the Universe. It was inaugurated in December, 1921 as a registered public body which adopted a constitution of its own.

A year before his death Tagore appealed to Mahatma Gandhi, through a letter dated 19 Feb 1940, to take a closer interest in Visva-Bharati, which he said was:

> … [A] vessel carrying the cargo of my life's best treasure and I hope it may claim special care from my countrymen for its preservation.

Gandhi replied the same day, saying, 'You may depend upon my doing all I can in the common endeavour to assure it permanence', adding, 'Visva-Bharati is a national institution. It is undoubtedly also international'. Prime Minister Jawaharlal Nehru, speaking in the Parliament of India, 3 May 1951, expressed:

> We have looked upon Visva-Bharati not only as a very great institution but as a very special and unique institution and we are particularly anxious that it should not fall into the rut of other universities….

Left: *Old Patha-Bhavana*
Right: *Siksha-Satra*

Consequently, it was declared a Central University and an institution of national importance in May, 1951 by an Act of Parliament.

Tagore's approach to education was remarkable—education begins in primary school and like the roots of a tree, grows into flourishing branches and leaves that constitute the university. Thus 'Patha-Bhavana' and 'Siksha-Satra' were born as the base of V-B, from where students evolved directly to university level—an astonishing idea indeed.

There is a picture of Gurudev himself taking a Patha-Bhavana class. Several other eminent scholars of V-B including Vice-Chancellors, such as the late Ashin Dasgupta, had taught in Patha-Bhavana. Many illustrious sons of the world, such as Amartya Sen, had studied there.

Studying in Patha-Bhavana also meant being close to nature. Thus, through classes held outside—underneath trees—students were exposed to an environment that naturally arouses curiosity about nature, seasonal changes, orientation of the sun and the moon, photosynthesis, animal behaviour, weather patterns, ecology…What better way can there be than the understanding of science in its most rudimentary form?

'Kuthibari' was bought by Tagore in 1912—nine years before V-B was established, so that students from Santiniketan could go and work in villages surrounding Surul, for rural reconstruction. Today, it forms the nucleus of Sriniketan in general, and 'Siksha-Satra' in particular, for providing hands-on training to rural students on pottery, weaving, textiles, electrical services-cum-maintenance, and rural biotechnology.

LEFT: *Playground of Siksha-Satra*
RIGHT: *Open-air classes of Ananda Pathshala*

Bauls in Poush Mela

Siksha-Satra is a further exemplification of Tagore's concern for the neighbouring villages. He felt the university must reach out to the surrounding habitats and propagate the message of 'vocational education', and thus *inter alia* expand the scope for employability of rural children.

Tagore believed that education was a vehicle for emancipation of mind and that this process could not be confined to just blackboard teaching of arts and science subjects. Thus every student had an exposure to cultural aspects of life, involving music, painting, sculptures, etc.; and here is why I call Visva-Bharati 'a real university'—a place where it is possible for an undergraduate student to take, for instance, courses in linguistics, computer science, music, painting and even theoretical physics!

Tagore was deeply influenced by Mustafa Jalaluddin Rumi, who was born in Kabul but lived in Shiraz of Persia (Iran), about 800 years ago. Rumi, the founder of 'Sufi' philosophy, had great influence on Tagore, who made two visits to Iran. I suspect his deep interest in 'bauls' of Birbhum and introduction of 'Baul Sangeet' as a part and parcel of 'Poush Mela' had emanated from Rumi's idea of Sufism. Today, no student is expected to come out of V-B without an appreciation of Baul Sangeet!

Those of you who have read Tagore's *Visva Parichay* or his conversations with the great physicist Albert Einstein, will be aware of his deep interest in science. In particular, while Einstein was a reluctant believer in quantum mechanics, Tagore had, astonishingly, an open-mindedness to its ramifications. Even without any formal training in science he raised issues of 'observables', 'wave-particle duality', etc. Thus, Tagore viewed science not as a subject disjointed from liberal arts and music, but as a complementary pursuit of knowledge.

In the discussion with Einstein, Tagore borrowed from 'Upanishada' which lays stress on 'Aham'—the self and its interaction with the Creator. It is this constant linkage between the self and nature that characterises the marvel of creation.

Tagore extends the notion of importance of the self and its interaction with the Creator to less-evolved creatures as well. He talks about vibration and energy dormant in every being in nature—large or small.

The Poet's thoughts on science and scientific concepts, in the context of the recent exploration of the Higgs Boson or the God Particle, is the subject of further discussion. These ideas find form in *Visva Parichay* which he wrote about four to five years before he passed away. At the twilight of Gurudev's life several scientific discoveries had activated his mind.

In the preface to *Visva Parichay,* which has been translated here, the Poet writes affectionately to his young colleague Satyendra Nath Bose:

> Any educated person must enter the arena of science if not the core of science, and in this regard, it is no shame to take the help of Literature…I am not a serious student of science but I had this endless temptation for tasting the juice of science from my very childhood….
>
> I was then about twelve when I had gone with my revered father to the Dalhousie hills. After the day's hard work we would settle on a divan in the veranda….
>
> The sun provides a curtain of light around our Earth and therefore we are unable to visualise the universe beyond, during the day. The day ends, the sun sets, the lid of light disappears, and it is then innumerable stars lit up the dark sky….

I could realise that the boundary of the universe extends far beyond our earth. Gradually, and beyond the periphery of mountain peaks, underneath the blue clear sky descend the stars. Father would introduce me to them, to the planets. Not merely an introduction but he would also tell me the distance of their orbits from the sun, the time period of revolution….

Amongst the stars in the middle of the night sky one finds patches of light plastered around, called the 'Milky Way'. Powerful telescopes have revealed that the Milky Way comprises billions of stars—there is really nothing called darkness. Those which are invisible also possess light. There is incessant emanation of radiation of different colours, even from the dark ends of the universe….

Though a far distance away, stars make their presence felt through light—some visible, some however invisible to the naked eye—question then arose: what is the mode of travel of light? The answer is a fascinating story—light travels as waves. It is difficult to fathom the nature of this wave.

Left: *Satyendra Nath Bose*
Right: *Young Robi taking lessons from father Maharshi Debendranath Tagore*

Concomitantly, however, another piece of data brought out a contrasting picture of light—that light consists of innumerable corpuscles or tiny particles. Experiments suggested that these light corpuscles are like a shower of very minute objects, which in today's parlance are called Bosons, after the name of their discoverer, Satyendra Nath Bose. About waves and particles, the Poet asks:

Rabindranath in deep comtemplation about the universe

> How does one reconcile these two apparently contradictory picturisation of light? What is more mind-boggling is that while the external manifestation of light is either as a wave or a particle, what appears in the micro world is neither this nor that—we call it radiation....
>
> ...One of the most bewildering entities of modern science is the little, hidden universe within our grand universe—and this is the atomic world. This tiny world is invisible to us but is at the very root of all creations.

Physicists now have found ways of breaking open the seemingly impregnable doors of atoms to reveal sub-atoms—namely electrons and protons. Tagore further writes:

> Let me now give the example of the lightest of atoms, namely hydrogen. At the centre of the hydrogen atom resides an electrically charged particle, called proton—and in the orbit of the proton revolves a single electron. Proton is positively charged while the electron is negatively charged. The negative electron is itinerant while the positive proton is heavy and static.

Recently scientists have discovered the antiparticle of electron, called the positron, which has the same mass of electron but is positively charged. Of course, Tagore did not live to see the discovery of the anti-proton, an object of great interest in the recent CERN experiments in Geneva. Gurudev further averred in *Visva Parichay*:

> The fact that an atom is disintegrable has prompted scientists to devise machines that can penetrate inside the atom…These machines send radiation deep inside the atom to probe its internal structure.

The Large Hadron Collider in Geneva is indeed a successor to the machines that Tagore had alluded to. In the CERN experiment physicists are busy studying the collisions of protons and antiprotons moving at extremely high speeds. The question is: What is providing the binding between the quarks that constitute the proton? Just as the light particle or photon, which is a Boson, provides the binding between the proton and the electron, a hidden Boson called the Higgs Boson is thought to provide the binding between the quarks.

In pursuance of Tagorean ideas of *Visva Parichay*, let me venture to emulate the great man by stating in simple terms the meaning of Symmetry and Symmetry-Breaking that endows quarks with mass. A quark can exist in two equivalent symmetry states, akin to the twin-brothers, Luv and Kush in our epic *Ramayana*.

Quarks are endowed with colour, but Luv and Kush are identical with no mass-difference. Then, how can we distinguish between them? Enters the plot the sage Balmiki, who is so far hidden under white termites, and who presents Luv with earrings. Now, there is no problem in separating him from Kush—the symmetry has been broken. In the process Luv acquires additional mass. Simultaneously, Balmiki also gets to be exposed—and that is the Higgs Boson-like particle discovered recently in CERN.

It is 'taranga' (vibration) that captured the imagination of Gurudev, in his identification with nature, universe, science and indeed his ideals of

Rabindranath Tagore teaching in Patha-Bhavana

education. Vibration, in quantum mechanics, is energy, and the latter is equivalent to mass, in accordance with the Theory of Relativity. Mass is an attribute of particulate matter while vibration is wave, which is the essence of wave-particle duality. What we perceive in this material world is matter, whereas that perception sends waves in our brain through neurons. It is the vibration of these waves which the Poet calls 'nritya', the cosmic dance of Nataraja, either in the context of the big bang or its simulation in the large hadron collider, as enshrined in CERN, Geneva.

Visva-Bharati in the Contemporary World

(Based on the original Bengali version, written jointly with Indrani Mukhopadhyay, that appeared in *Chaturanga*, 71 year of publication, No.1, Baisakh-Ashad (August 2014). The songs of Rabindranath, cited in this discussion, are included in *Gitabitan.)*

At this point of time—when we are about to start preparation for the centenary celebration of the great man's remarkable creation, Visva-Bharati (V-B)—the question that naturally arises is: how contextually important are Gurudev's ideals, methods of holistic education, institutions, built on Upanishadic concepts and his conscious efforts to harmonise with nature?

After Gurudev's death, in the wake of the gradual disappearance of innumerable entities that marked the progress of the new world, new developments have taken place in consonance with present-day ideas. Tagore was not averse to adopting evolving thoughts and had embraced novel concepts by abandoning old ones, seeking amalgamation of the East's spiritualism with the advancement of Western science. Given this background, it is important to critically analyse the significance of Tagore's Visva-Bharati, as well as weigh the importance of his entire vision of education. His lifelong effort was directed at the creation of an institution like V-B that would see this union of East and West to strive to unify the self with the Creator via the marvel of nature.

Examining the disappearance of the telegram, the pen and the inkpot, the gramophone record, etc.—things with which Tagore had intimate and inseparable contact, but are now lost forever—help us reach important conclusions.

A news item appeared sometime back, seemingly innocuous but not without some significance: the abolition of the telegram. In this fast-moving world we do not even find the time for sending a facsimile in preference to the e-mail; what is then the import of the demise of the telegram? Well, a moment's reflection would reveal that a part of history had also been written off, along with the telegram. Our memory has to be rekindled with words like:

> FATHER SERIOUS STOP COME SHARP STOP
> JOB OFFERED STOP JOIN IMMEDIATELY STOP
> WIFE DELIVERED MALE ISSUE STOP MOTHER–CHILD FINE STOP

What role did the telegram play in Rabindranath's life? He cabled to son Rathindranath from Santiniketan in the summer of 1931:

> Daughter-in-Law is alright now. It will however be not wise to move her from here immediately. She ought to stay here at least until 15 July. If there is a sudden change of plans, do send a telegram to Ananga so that he reaches Calcutta.[2]

Again, later:

> Rathi—I learnt from Andrews' telegram that Neetu's condition has deteriorated…Amiya cabled today that he is coming—that will be some relief for me.[3]

We find in the sixth volume of *Rabijibani*:

> The Swedish Academy was unaware of the Poet's address. Perhaps because of that they used the medium of McMillan to officially write from London on 14 November, which we quote verbatim: XF PH LONDON PO 14 EASTNLN19

> RABINDRANATH TAGORE 6 DN TAGORE LANE JORASANKO CALCUTTA SWEDISH ACADEMY AWARDED YOU NOBEL PRIZE IN LITERATURE PLEASE WIRE ACCEPTATION SWEDISH MINISTER CALCUTTA/15 NO 13/GPO. On receipt, of this the Poet's son-in-law, Nagendranath, telegraphically informed Gurudev, on 16 November at 07:10 hours: FOLLOWING CABLE RECEIVED MIDNIGHT STOP SWEDISH ACADEMY AWARDS YOU NOBEL PRIZE IN LITERATURE STOP PLEASE WIRE ACCEPTATION STOP SWEDISH MINISTER STOP NAGEN.

Upon hearing this news, numerous followers and friends of the Poet inundated him with telegraphic messages, the first of which read thus:

> HANDED IN AT CALCUTTA 14 AT 16:10 RECD HERE AT 16:43 STOP RABINDRANATH TAGORE STOP SANTINIKETAN STOP BOLPUR STOP NOBEL PRIZE CONFERRED ON YOU STOP OUR CONGRATULATIONS STOP MANILAL SATYENDRA CHARU.

This means the telegram that was sent at 16:10 by Manilal Gangopadhyay, Satyandranath Datta and Charuchandra Bondyopadhyay to Rabindranath, congratulating him on the award of the Nobel Prize, reached the Bolpur Post and Telegraph office at 16:43.[4] In response to the telegram from Rothenstein congratulating the Poet on the Nobel Prize he wired him on 18 November:

> The very first moment I received the message of the great honour conferred on me by the award of the Nobel Prize my heart turned towards you with love and gratitude. I felt certain that of all my friends none would be more glad at this news than you. But, all the same, it is a very great trial for me. The

> perfect whirlwind of public excitement it has given rise to is frightful. It is almost as bad as tying a tin can at a dog's tail making it impossible for him to move without creating noise and collecting crowds all along. I am being smothered with telegrams and letters for the last few days and the people who never read a line of my works are loudest in their protestations of joy.[5]

Once again:

> Dear son, I forward to you the cablegram from Elmhirst from which you will know the details. I note that you have cabled him to his home address which will not reach him.[6]

Not just the telegram, even postcards, inland letters, aerograms, etc., have been reduced to museum pieces. It is worth speculating on whether Gurudev would have at all written the remarkable short story called *Post Master* had he been alive today!

Leaving aside the electromagnetically transmitted telegrams and cablegrams, Rabindranath was deeply influenced too by the post-bearers (dak-harkara). Santidev Ghosh wrote in his book *Rabindrasangit*:

> For the Poet, Gagan-Harkara was his peon, the great 'baul'-exponent Lalan Fakir was his supplier of betel leaves and one of the sedan-carriers ('palki-wallah') was his Guru.[7]

The famous song of Gagan Harkara, *Ami Kothai Pabo Tare,* was adopted by the Poet to *Amaar Shonar Bangla,* which is the national anthem of Bangladesh today.

Along with the abolition of letter-writing we also see the disuse of the pen and the inkpot, based on which Gurudev wrote a heart-warming short story 'Apad', from which we translate a few lines:

> Satish brought a fancy inkstand from Calcutta. It is flanked on both sides by two small boat-shaped conch shell pots and adorned in the middle by a swan made of German silver, which balances a pen in between its spread-out wings. Satish was very fond of this contraption, his fondness being evident from the care with which he would dust the equipment with a silk handkerchief. Kiran would make fun of this by stroking the swan's beak and muttering, 'You—the king of swans—how could you be reduced to this state from your Brahminical lineage!' Exchanges like this would become topics of friendly banters between her and the brother-in-law Satish.[8]

Tagore wrote to Rathindranath from New Haven, Connecticut on 24 October 1930:

> Please bring copious amounts of coloured ink and paper—the latter from Germany—but note that France produces the best quality ink. However, remember to bring large bottles, lest they are emptied soon.[9]

On 21 November of 1930, the Poet wrote to his son:

> Professor Formichi had come; He is still sincerely attracted towards us Indians. Upon seeing me tears started rolling down from his eyes. I asked him if it would be alright if I return to India via Italy. He replied that a simple letter to Mussolini would clear all complexities. I told him that I would write. I am enclosing that letter to you. If you agree, please post that letter—it is not good to keep alive the animosity with Italy. I am not quite sure of how to write an Italian address—it is perhaps like this: II Duce / Signor Mussolini.[10]

In the short story named 'Khata', Rabindranath writes, and we translate:

> Uma has become a pain since the time she learnt how to write. She is tirelessly inscribing on all the walls in oblique and oversized letters the following lines: *Jal Parey, Pata Narey.* Uma's presumptuous elder-brother Gobindalal had written a voluminous essay on the apparent misconceptions about physiology, prevalent in certain European scientists, employing bombastic language, devoid of logic. On one lonely afternoon Uma took her brother's ink and pen to scribble in large letters on the hapless essay: Gopal is a very good boy. He does not mind savouring whatever is fed to him![11]

Nearly seventy five years on, following the Poet's passing, we frantically run after various modern versions of cell phones—our lives seeming pointless without the possession of the latest in the series; letter–writing being relegated to the quick messaging system so hasty in nature that we do not even have the time to spell out 'are 'and 'you' which have become 'r' and 'u'. The simplicity and the easy pace of Tagore's world eludes us today.

Concurrent with the demise of the telegram came the heart-rending news of the winding-up, of the park street shop—'Music World', because no one used the gramophone records anymore. Yet, its omnipresence during Tagore's time finds reflection in many of his writings. In a letter to son Rathindranath from Bremen, Germany, on 5 October 1930, the Poet wrote:

> Do read the letter of Bake. My songs have now found ways of appropriate preservation and presentation to the general public. They are now going to use Ediphone for recording my songs. This will finally speed up the process of recording. We might ourselves try to procure this instrument if we can generate resources.[12]

Gurudev wrote to the great music exponent Dilip Kumar Roy (the son of Dwijendralal Roy), the translation of which reads:

> I am satisfied with the way you sang 'Hey Kshaniker Atithee'—in your own style, though you took a bit of liberty of expression keeping intact however my melody. I have no objection to your recording this song in a gramophone.[13]

In *Sur O Sangati* we find reference to the exchange between Rabindranath and Dhurjotiprasad Mukhopadhyay:

> The voice of 'New Bengal' may be more primitive than that of the gramophone but as long as it does not sound like 'His Master's Voice'—as long as it can improvise on his own tune, it will justify its existence.[14]

We are so used to listening to FM radio today that we have almost forgotten the presence of the medium wave, though our childhood memories are centred on valve radios, preceding the discovery of the transistor in the fifties.

On radio, Prabhatkumar Mukhopadhyay wrote in *Mongpute Ekmas*, which when translated reads:

> The mysterious radio waves, carrying a variety of melodies from far distances seem to mesmerise the Poet. He was so smitten by them that he was inspired to pen the poem 'Manasi' on the lonely banks of the river Padma while listening to the radio, as narrated by the Poet to Maitreyi Devi.[15]

We find in Amal Home's *Smritikatha*:

> I recall seeing hordes of people crowding the lane leading from Cornwallis Street to Hemendramohan's house where the Poet would come to record his songs. And we the youngsters would wait in excited expectation at the Basu-residence. Our delight would reach unexpected heights when Gurudev would make multiple attempts for achieving perfection, such as for recording

> the song 'Vande Mataram'. Alas, many of these records, especially of the patriotic songs that were sung with powerfully deep voice of Gurudev, have been ruined with time. Had these records been accessible today they would have been a testimony to how forceful his voice was.[16]

This dramatic shift in our lifestyle brought about by technology finds expression in Gurudev's own writings. In the Poet's words:

> We should not be drowned in superficial excitement that is transient and is like a mirage. We should energise our inner strength. Even a fleeting recognition of our inner vibration can stay with us forever. If we can be true to our own selves, even momentarily, then truth will stay immortal and will sow the indestructible seed of salvation permanently in our lies.[17]

However, Gurudev was not averse to change and in fact pre-empted it in a very positive manner, recognising the fact that every generation had its own unique challenges and rewards. There were several instructions, directions and examples that had been left for posterity by Gurudev—attributes that are timeless and are indeed of immense importance and relevance to us even today.

If we look into education in the backdrop of Gurudev's own concept of it, which hinges on its all-encompassing, complementary and seamless forms, we realise V-B as a university, combining the best of both East and West and open to the entire world, is a far-reaching idea in itself. Our Ministry of Human Resource and Development has been goading all central universities of late to incorporate schools within their premises. The shape of such schools is envisaged to be different from Kendriya Vidyalayas or Central schools. The latter, though situated within the campuses, are not organically and symbiotically bonded with the universities. It is felt that even professors of the university should descend to school level to familiarise young students with the fruits of their research work. It is interesting to note that Gurudev had visualised such Ashram-based schools that the Ministry is talking about, more than a century ago!

In addition, the central universities are being urged to open 'community colleges' to bring adjoining village folks within the fold of the educational systems. Once again, it is amusing to see history being repeated here, as Gurudev had conceptualised and initiated 'Siksha-Satra', Rural Reconstruction Project and 'Patha-Chakra' a long time ago. If we can rejuvenate these newly evolving ideas of school education and community college within the existing system of V-B, the latter can become a model university, which our founding father had desired.

Tagore's unbelievably modern thoughts on science had taken a path breaking turn as far as education was concerned. He felt familiarity with rudimentary science had to be inculcated from childhood by citing examples from the fascinating presence of nature. That is why Gurudev planned to hold classes outside, under trees, in the midst of nature so that small children could be made to be aware of seasonal changes, orientations of the sun and the moon, basic plant science, ecology etc. The social behaviour of insects such as ants, bees, wasps, etc.—how they form colonies—are all parts of modern Entomology. But we can easily associate our Patha-Bhavan and Siksha-Satra students with these modern views by employing nature as a laboratory!

Tagore wrote in *Visva Parichay*:

> The legend has it that one of the greatest scientists Newton once witnessed an apple falling from a tree. A query travelled across his inquisitive mind—why does the fruit descend downwards and not ascend upwards? Along with that came the question: what makes the moon revolve around the earth, or for that matter, why does the earth orbit around the sun? Through the observation of the falling apple he surmised that the mother earth has power of attraction—it draws every object towards its centre. If that is so, why should the moon behave differently? This force of attraction must be applicable to all entities, far and near! Larger the mass content stronger is the strength of attraction.[17]

Santiniketan and Sriniketan skies are relatively pollution-free. Hence, the manner in which Tagore took his first lesson on the cosmos can easily be introduced to our school children. The priceless information contained in *Visva Parichay* is astonishingly modern. We might find it rather amusing in the background of our propensity to ape Western science that we are blessed with year-long climatic conditions that make nature our laboratory, a facility that cold and frozen climes of the West do not permit!

It is ironic that we are today lapping up borrowed ideas from the West that point to the incompleteness of education, if it is restricted to just science or social studies. The best American universities mandatorily require their post-graduate science students to credit courses in Music or Arts. But that is precisely what Gurudev had desired so that V-B pass-outs could evolve as healthy, sensitive and good citizens of the world at large. He had repeatedly stressed on borderless education that does not erect partitions between subjects. In his own words: I never envisaged education to be fragmented.[18] When all the top universities of the globe are in the process of introducing interdisciplinary studies, such as across the topics of biology, chemistry and physics, why should we in V-B be drawn into regimentation in education?

During our visit to China in the recent past, we were impressed to note that its citizenry, young and old, frequent the parks, fields and street corners, in the afternoons and involve themselves in dances and limb-movements, along with music. The intimate connection between music and rejuvenation of the body and the mind is indeed what is reflected in our dance-form, practised in 'Briksharopan' and 'Basantotsav'. Similarly, our minds are filled with joy when we witness the Kala-Bhavana students engaging themselves in painting and sketching out in the open, illustrating the Bard's far-sighted concepts of an all-encompassing education.

Tagore's universally relevant and time-immemorial messages on the continuity of life are reassuring. Though many objects may have disappeared from our lives, what ushers in hope is this undying Ashramic philosophy of daily existence. We translate one of his 'upasana' speeches:

> Today all my voids in life are filled with delight, as I feel the all-pervasive presence of Him. The losses I have suffered have not diminished a bit what I have gained from Him. This world has not been able to take away any inner possessions of mine, several deaths around me have not minimised me in front of You, and the limitless universe has been unable to denude me—not even a single molecule or an atom of my existence. He is omnipresent in my life with His eternal blessing.[19] That is why, whatever decays or diminishes in this world reappears in immortal manifestations, in this Ashram-life.[20]

In another discourse to a congregation, the Poet had mentioned that there are two distinct tunes which emanate from this Ashram—one is the 'Tune of Humanity' and the other is the 'Tune of Nature'. We may interpret this deep statement as follows: The 'Tune of Humanity' embraces the disciplines of Humanities, Arts and Music while the 'Tune of Nature' embeds all of sciences including environmental studies. We may even underline the fact that life in the Ashram is itself an art.

Rabindranath wanted to propagate the Gayatri Mantra, in which the basics of physics and biology are hidden. Savitri, the sun-goddess, is the foundational deity of our universe from the energy of whom we derive our life, mind and soul. The sum and substance of Gurudev's discourses in our 'Upasana Griha' is that energy and light are the bridge between our conscious and sub-conscious. The last portion of *Visva Parichay* also elaborates on this deep concept for assimilation in our own mind. What is remarkable to comprehend from the above-mentioned upasanas and the concluding chapter of *Visva Parichay* is the symbiotic relation between science and spiritualism that Tagore had established through his songs and writings. One of the examples of this symbiosis can be found in the song *Tahare Aroti Kore Chandrotopon* in the Swaralipi-based book of *Baitalik* by Dinendranath Tagore.

Needless to say, our Baitalik-mantra Om pita nohsi and the Gayatri-mantra Om bhur bhuvah swaha are both taken from our ancient 'Suklayajur' Veda. The word 'taken' may imply extraction but the more important point is that our entire existentialistic facet is embedded in the Veda. Indeed, the reference to 'Pita' in Baitalik-mantra as well as to human consciousness in Gayatri-mantra are inscribed in Suklayajur Veda.

The Upasana-mantra, imbibed from 'Swetaswatara' Upanishad, chanted in the evenings, brings out a further awareness of the Ashramic value-system. It translates to mean:

> Salutations to the Divinity who is in the fire, who is in the water, who is in plants, who is in the tress, who has pervaded the whole universe.[21]

Appropriate versions of this mantra can be found in many Rabindrasangeets like: *Mor shondhaai tumi shundoro beshe eshechho; Shondhaa holo go-o maa; Bhubaneswar hey,* etc.

Our upasana traditions, which have been in existence from the Vedic era, had Rabindranath Tagore as the heir-embodiment of generations of rishi-disciples who had venerated the appearance of the Almighty out of darkness to bring enlightenment. That is why the rishis of the Aryan traditions had prayed to this omnipotent figure—not for wealth, recognition, happiness or acquisition, but to know Him, to unite with Him in order to be blessed with the nectar which is 'deathless'. It is He, the all-pervasive and omnipresent great soul who lives amongst us, and helps unify the human-awareness.

We should also mention here the morning upasana that is complementary to the evening one, discussed above, which is based on Brihadaranyaka Upanishad. What is that prayer? It says:

> Oh, Thee—take me from the untruth to the truth, to the illumination from the darkness; Oh, the Greatest of greats—please let your benevolent face and kind looks befall on me.

These words had been uttered by Maitreyi who had accompanied her husband Jajnavalkya to 'Vanaprastha'. The words are not to be merely chanted but must be absorbed and internalised by everyone of this Ashram.

One other eternal message of truth from the Swetaswatara Upanishad, which is a timeless and essential ingredient of the Ashram-life, is always sung during our yearly convocations. The root meaning of the verse[22] is:

> He who is the God of all gods—the Lord of this universe, is the one who is to be always worshipped. Those who get to know him acquire immortality.

Despite the fact that a university imparts knowledge in various fields of arts, humanities and sciences, our understanding is incomplete if we do not come to grips with the Almighty. All our educational pursuit would come to nought if we do not get to comprehend the Creator.

The next stanza of the above verse translates to read thus:

> He has nothing to achieve for Himself nor has He any organ of action. No one is seen equal or superior to Him. His great power alone is described in the Vedas to be of various kinds, and His knowledge, strength and action are described as inherent in Him.

The source and the cause of all of philosophy and science, be it in the material or the spiritual world, are one and the same. Schopenhauer has effectively discussed this fact in his book *Principle of Sufficient Reason.* Though he has identified Will and Idea as the two drivers of this world, he has put Will above Idea as the main motivating factor. It is then interesting to enquire what our verse from Swetaswatara Upanishad says in this context: The Creator is not shackled by the relation between the cause and the effect—His presence is beyond this effect. His wisdom, force and play emanate quite naturally. Through this word 'naturally' is conveyed the notion of spontaneity, which is above the cause and the effect. Therefore, it is not the material thing but the awareness of the material world that must be absorbed by all of us.

> No one in the world is His master, nor has anybody any control over Him. There is no sign by which He can be inferred.

> His is the cause of all, and the ruler of individual souls. He has no parent, nor is there anyone who is His lord. He is not endowed with a master or a driver—He himself is the mover of His chariot. He has no father, no mother—He himself is the superior soul, moulded into one who has no gender, neither of the father nor the mother. He who has spread himself all over in this universe is the one who is at the core of our spiritual enlightenment. On the one hand, He is the Emperor of this universe and on the other, also the Lord of our soul. He who will comprehend Him fully through scholarship and dedication would acquire the eventual salvation.

Though Rabindranath's multi-dimensional talent, profound spiritualism and the enormity of his far-sighted imagination are beyond comprehension by mere mortals, deep inside he was like a child, full of simplicity and straightforwardness and that is why he had thought of education to grow from the very beginning, like a flowering tree. On his seventieth birthday: 25 Baisakh of 1338, the Poet wrote and we translate:

> At the conclusion of my long journey around the circle of my life, when the end is near, I have come to understand one basic fact and that is I am just a poet…I am not a learned theorist nor a leader of ideas—some have called me a wise man, some have put me on the pedestal of a school master. But from the very childhood I had been more attracted towards games and had avoided school masters—the post of a school master does not suit me. At this ripe age I feel it is futile to claim greatness or adjudge myself as superior or inferior to others; I do not care for recognition from people who have been busy devising various methods of evaluation. I do not want to strive for small crumbs of rewards and I wish that my mind does not get cluttered by hankering for various yardsticks of success.[23]

He further wrote:

> My gratification, my pleasure are derived from inducing and encouraging small children into music and dance, which are in harmony with the rhythm of the Nataraj. I do not wish to embark on more sombre pursuits. I want to loudly pronounce to those who want to ceremonially elevate me to greater heights that having been born in this mother earth as an ordinary being I endeavour to remain enmeshed on the soil and the grass surrounding the plants and trees of this beautiful world. I want to declare myself as a poet—a friend of those who have their undistinguished initiation in this world as ordinary human beings, who start to learn treading on this earth and meet their eventual (and inevitable) demise within this mother earth itself.[24]

Rabindranath in Chhatimtala

In conclusion, this essay is a portrayal of the old and the new, the transient and the endless, the vanquished and the resurrected, the mortal and the immortal, in the backdrop of Gurudev's own life and philosophy. The Tagorean model of education in itself is an exemplification of what may be considered a timeless ideal that has not lost its relevance in this fast moving world.

Endnotes

1. Rabindranath Tagore, *Chithipatra*, second part, (Kolkata: Visva-Bharati Granthana Vibhaga, 1942), p.208
2. Ibid., p. 209
3. Prasantakumar Pal, *Rabijibani*, vol.6, (Kolkata: Ananda Publishers Pvt. Ltd,1993) pp. 443–444
4. Ibid., p.445
5. Rabindranath Tagore, *Chithipatra*, second part, p. 209
6. Santidev Ghosh, *Rabindrasangit*, (Kolkata: Visva-Bharati Granthana Vibhaga, 1970), p. 102
7. Rabindranath Tagore, *Rabindra-Rachanavali*, vol. 19, (Kolkata: Visva-Bharati Granthana Vibhaga,1988), p. 275
8. Rabindranath Tagore, *Chithipatra*, second part, p. 198
9. Ibid., p.204
10. Rabindranath Tagore, *Rabindra-Rachanavali*, vol. 18, (Kolkata: Visva-Bharati Granthana Vibhaga, 1966), pp. 317–318
11. Rabindranath Tagore, *Chithipatra*, second part, p. 195
12. Rabindranath Tagore, *Sangitchinta,*(Kolkata:Visva-Bharati Granthana Vibhaga,1985) p. 123
13. Ibid., p. 167
14. Prabhatkumar Mukhopadhyay, *Rabindrajibani*, (Kolkata: Visva-Bharati Granthana Vibhaga, 2014), pp. 188–189
15. *Ek Dui Tin*, (Rabindra Sangeet Smritikatha, Amal Home,) pp. 8–9
16. Rabindranath Tagore, *Santiniketan,* second part, (Kolkata: Visva-Bharati Granthana Vibhaga 1991), p. 234
17. Ibid., p. 380
18. Santidev Ghosh, *Rabindranather Purnanga Sikshadarsa—Sangeet O Nritya*, (Kolkata, Ananda Publishers Pvt. Ltd), p.16
19. Rabindranath Tagore, *Santiniketan*, second part, p. 153
20. Ibid., p. 151
21. Swami Tyagisananda, *Swetaswatara Upanishad*, (Sri Ramkrishna Math), p. 60
22. Swami Tyagisananda, *Swetaswatara Upanishad*, pp. 96–125
23. *Prabasi*, pp. 5–6
24. Ibid., p.6

Man and Nature

Gurudev Rabindranath Tagore spent his lifetime exploring the theme of Man and Nature through his poems, songs, paintings and indeed all his creative endeavours. A photograph of Gurudev in our Chhatimtala when he permanently moved to Santiniketan at exactly the midpoint of his lifetime, at 40 years of age, shows him under a large tree, craving to find solace in the midst of nature just as he was seeking the meaning of our existence.

The Man-Nature interface is actually one of a Trinity in which the Creator is at the apex. The Creator or the Creation through a phenomenon called the Big Bang had given rise to both Man and Nature, and hence the interfacing of these two entities would inevitably have to relate to the Almighty There is no better way of doing this than through the numerous songs of Tagore.

How did Rabindranath address this issue? Well, he incorporated it within a curriculum that gave birth to a remarkable model of education that is so topical in today's troubled world. He began a Brahmacharya Ashram in 1901 in Santiniketan, geographically far away from the British Calcutta, so as to begin afresh a form of education that will be free from the shackles of imperial biases and will be rooted in our ancient Eastern thoughts, emanating from the Upanishads and the Vedas. He introduced outdoor classes so that the disciples would imbibe the rudimentary scientific concepts of the Man-Nature interface.

There is a picture of a teacher taking a class in the Brahmacharya Ashram that eventually grew into today's Patha-Bhavana. There were no blackboard teachings but animated discourses that included music, dance, painting, etc. The Basantotsav is one such important event in the V-B calendar that institutionalises Gurudev's idea of holistic education which incorporates in a ritualistic manner the onset of the beautiful season of spring. Students' educational excursions were designed within the curriculum to further enhance the awareness amongst the young children about the marvel of nature. In fact, one of the reasons behind Tagore's decision to create a university in Birbhum was indeed the sharply discerning changes that you witness with every change of season: summer, monsoon, autumn, fall, winter and spring.

The season of summer (*grishma*) in Birbhum is scorchingly oppressive as you would be able to detect through this song:

'Darun agnibaane re / Hhriday trishaa haane re…'

Amid the scorching intense Sun the heart pines for thirst

However, Gurudev found enchanting beauty and salvation—through nature—because hot summer days were followed by Norwesters when:

'Jibon jokhon shukhai jai / Karunadharay esho…'

(When life is parched dry, do appear as shower of mercy)

Left: *Teacher taking class in Brahmachrya Ashram*
Right: *Today's Chhatimtala*

The rainy season (*varsha*), like the spring, evoked romantic responses when the Poet penned numerous songs: *Megher pore megh jomechhe*...; *Aji Srabonoghono gahono mohe*...; *Aji jhoro jhoro mukhoro bador-dine*... and so on.

Suddenly one fine morning the sky cleared and one observed white clouds in the background of the captivating blue sky—the *sharada* had arrived, the message being reflected on the ground by picturesque *kashbons*: *Amra bendhechhi kasher guchho*...

The autumn ended and brought in its wake the fall season (*hemanta)*, which in a way combined a bit of three seasons, namely the autumn, winter and spring, and that found expression in: *Hemonte kon boshonter bani*...

Bolpur, being about 160 kms north of Kolkata, faces a severe winter (*shishir*), when the temperature in Sriniketan drops to about 4 degrees celsius, inspiring the Bard to write: *Sheeter haoyar laglo nachon amlokir ei dale daale / Pataguli shirshiriye*...

Finally, the crescendo—the Queen of all Seasons—the spring (*vasanta*) that figures in Tagore's innumerable love songs: '*Boshonte phul ganthlo amar joyer mala, bailo prane dokhin haoya, agunjala*...; *Aji dokhino duar khola*...*esho hey*...*amar boshonto esho*...; *Aha aaji e boshonte eto phul phote, eto pakhi gaye*...

Gurudev attempted to engrave in the minds of the V-B fraternity the significance of the Man-Nature interface by institutionalising structured functions (*utsavs*) as part of regular academic activities of the university. A glimpse of that background concept can be had from *Visva Parichay* (An Introduction to the Universe), written by the Poet in fluid Bengali prose between 1934 and 1937. While discussing the evolution of our Mother Earth Tagore writes:

> The gradual cooling of the hot lump that the earth was, yielded a congenial atmosphere, ready to lead to water bodies and forests. Then came birds, animals and finally human beings. In the beginning Man used to meet his daily needs from products of the forests. Afterwards the acquired use of fire enabled him to eat the meat of the hunted animals. The medieval man was then a resident of the forest. However, the need of habitats grew with

the growth of human population. Man started chopping trees, cleaning up jungles in order to create homes for himself. Pity, the same forest which had so far nourished man became its victim, with the concomitant decline of the quality of the environment.

The leaves of the tree help generating oxygen from the sunlight through the process of photosynthesis. The tree roots assist in binding the earth that helps arrest avalanches and earthquakes, but alas, the trees became items of sacrifice because of human greed. That is why Gurudev wanted to make us conscious of the vital importance of trees by introducing 'Briksharopan' which we now celebrate on 22 Sravan, the day of Tagore's passing, when we sing in chorus:

> *Morubijoyar keton udao shunne, hey probol pran…*
> (Let the victory flag symbolising the conquering of arid desert land flutter in the open sky, ushering-in indomitable life)

The next in line is the complementary utsav of 'Halakarshan'—the ploughing of land. Fruits alone could not suffice; there would be need for agricultural produces through farming, hence was the necessity of ploughing. The chosen site for this event by Tagore and his illustrious son Rathindranath, was naturally Sriniketan, the soil of which was selected for locating the institutes of Agricultural Sciences and Rural Extension Centre. The 'Halakarshan' concept is epitomised by the songs:

> *Amra chash kori anondey; Shob kajey hathlagai mora shob kajei…*
> (We plough our land in happiness; we must lend our helping hand in all kinds of labour)

Briksharopan and Halakarshan functions have assumed enormous contemporary significance because of denuding of forests and consequent degradation of the environment, rampantly visible today.

The Man-Nature interface is further exemplified by another remarkable festival also celebrated in Sriniketan, namely 'Shilpotsav'. The latter is an event that reminds us of the important contributions of our village artisans in designing metal tools that eventually feed into factory machines. Man derives resources by mining iron ores, which are then converted into rust-free steel by inserting, in limited amounts, Nitrogen or Oxygen into iron.

The Poet writes:

> *Kothheen loha kothheen ghume chilo ocheton, o tar ghum bhangayinu re*
> (The rigid iron ore remained a sleepy, lifeless lump, let us awaken it to application)

Given this background it is pertinent to remind ourselves of our Founder's message on how we ought to continue to remain vigilant about the conservation and preservation of nature. Today our energy needs are making deep onslaughts onto the nature—the exhausts from automobiles are leading to increased air pollution and holes in the Ozone-layer, excessive pumping of water from the earth-bed is causing more-than-tolerable levels of arsenic and fluorides in water, extensive use of plastics is clogging the drainage system thus leading to flooding of streets during high rainfalls, deforestation is triggering erosion of soils thereby causing devastating floods, indiscriminate cutting of mangroves is giving rise to enhanced Tsunami-damages, and so on. That is why we feel it is time that we pay renewed attention in V-B to environmental sciences including climate studies that will increase awareness in this enormously significant area of contemporary discourses. The subject is truly interdisciplinary as it requires amalgamation of various topics of geography, chemistry, metallurgy, biology and mathematical modelling. It is also important to sensitise the community through workshops and science-*yatras* in which Tagore's songs can play a very critical role. The Rural Extension Centre and our School of Education, namely Vinaya-Bhavana can act as nucleating centres to catalyse an interdisciplinary approach in which our Integrated Science program, Siksha-Bhavana, the departments of geography and computer science can all join together in a complementary endeavour. That will be a fitting tribute to Gurudev's vision of what this university ought to be like.

Responsibility of a Library

I am privileged to recall what our founder Gurudev Rabindranath Tagore had to say about the main responsibility of a library and its librarian. Two essays of Tagore, first in *Bichitra Prabandha,* which he wrote at the young age of twenty-four, and the other for the Presidential speech at the All-India Library Congress, which was delivered on his behalf in December 1928, when Gurudev was sixty-seven years old, explore this theme at great length.

I have taken several excerpts[1] from these two essays and summarised the essence of some of its text to enable my readers understand how Tagore visualised a library and the importance he gave to its librarian.

> A library can be thought of as a 'Tower of Silence'– like a sleeping child, which embodies the entrapped vibrations of an age-old ocean. Here, language is still, like a calm mass of water that has stopped flowing. Man's unbounded enlightenment, shackled with words, is imprisoned in the papers in black and white. If all these sublime aspirations of the quest of human mind suddenly find expression—if the rebellious words fly in all directions it will be akin to a torrent from the melted ice of the Himalayas. The library encloses within itself this very deluge of the ardent expressions of human souls.

Inside a library, we feel like standing at the crossroads of thousands of avenues. Some paths lead to infinite seas, some take us to endless peaks, and some penetrate deep inside the human heart. One may chart out in any of the multitudes of directions—without hindrance. Human emancipation is contained within the four-walls of the library.

Every day we receive innumerable missives from far and wide, encompassing the past and the future. Should we be reduced to simply copying these letters and publishing them in English newspapers? Should the names of my countrymen only adorn the second page of application forms? Should we subject ourselves to the subservient positions of fighting litigation cases over trivial matters of possessiveness? Let the library be the repository of the voice of Bengal—in consonance with the music of the world.

I now turn to Tagore's speech[2] in December 1928 at the All-India Library Congress, on the principal duty of a library.

One of man's main enemies is his propensity to be an accumulator. Once he starts collecting he gets intoxicated by the sheer number of his collections, forgetting the principal goal.

Most libraries are infected by the fad to accumulate. Almost three quarters of the collected books are not useful—the rest of the one-quarter gets submerged by the volume of the total number. Ironically, big libraries take pride in their big collections. Instead they should seek reputation in their ability to put their books to use.

The total number of words extant in our language can be put into two baskets: dictionary and literature. It is interesting to note that much of the words in big dictionaries are seldom employed. But they need to be there. On the other hand, words of literature are lively—each is indispensable. One must admit that literature is more valuable than dictionary.

Rabindranath in his study

Same thing can be said about the library. Success of the library is not measured by the books that occupy the shelves but by those which are variably perused, every day. Often a librarian gets carried away by an impressive array of collection—he forgets to put in the thought and hard work to make the library user-friendly, the reason being, by amassing something one can easily impress the common mind.

Ordinarily, libraries carry book-lists that are on routine display. But the lists are usually listless and unattractive. But the dividing line between good and average libraries is in the ability of the former in extending a warm welcome to the reader. This is what we call modesty which is the hallmark of great libraries—not in size but in character. It is not the reader who makes a library—it is the library that makes a reader.

If we remember this then it is evident that a good librarian has a task cut out for him. This job does not end by simply cataloguing the books in the shelves—he must have a feel for the books.

> But too big a library makes it unmanageable for the librarian. That is why I think big libraries are mainly storehouses. Smaller libraries on the other hand are ideal places to savour the goodies.
>
> What I understand by small libraries is that they must contain books of many departments but they must not lose their sharpness and attractiveness. Every book ought to have its own special feature. An ideal librarian therefore must be a true worshipper of knowledge, freed from the desire to mindlessly filling-up the shelves.

In the end, I want to reiterate the main points of this essay. In short, the principal aim of a library is to be user-friendly—and to enable the reader to be familiar and enthusiastic about the books. Its idea is not to be a mere accumulator and procurer of books.

These words were spoken by our Founder about nine decades ago, but they are still relevant. Had Gurudev been alive today he would have embraced modern developments of e-books and e-journals. With space becoming an issue it is imperative that libraries adopt the medium of electronic communication. Also, effective software must be implemented in order to have an efficient accession and cataloguing system. Thus, today's librarians must not be just deft procurers of books and journals—they ought to be good information officers as well.

Endnotes

1. Based on 'Library'—Bichtra Prabandha, Rabindra Rachanabali, Vol. 5, p 439
2. 'Janma Satabarshik Sanskaran', Paschim Bongo, Vol. 15, p 221

In Search of Convergence

Today, we face some challenges in balancing Tagore's ideals with the fast-paced, rapidly changing contemporary world and the expectations from central universities. There is need to not spread ourselves too thin and to focus on a few areas that mesh with Gurudev's visions, and yet have unique and modern relevance which will place Visva-Bharati (V-B) prominently in the world map as a beacon of cultural and educational innovation. This challenging task can be made a reality in V-B.

First, the Tagore model of holistic, borderless education that begins at the very roots of primary and secondary school education and eventually finds nourishment to develop into a fully grown tree, with masters and doctoral inputs from the arts and sciences, finds much interest in the present world. Visva-Bharati is not an Indian Institute of Technology (IIT), Indian Institute of Science (IISc), or an Indian Institute of Science Education and Research (IISER) or any other university with straight-jacketed and unidirectional emphases. It is a universal 'Ashram' from where the students emerge as complete human beings, ready to become good world citizens. It is interesting that our ministry (MHRD) is goading every central university to embed a school in its campus. We already have not just one, but four, for more than one hundred years, in the form of Ananda and Santosh 'Pathsalas' and secondary (and higher secondary) schools of Patha-Bhavana and Siksha-Satra.

Combined with this, we have begun a five year integrated course, after higher secondary, in which students can opt for courses in basic sciences, agricultural sciences as well as 'Kala' and 'Sangeet'. This possibility does not exist anywhere else in India, though some American and European universities are practicing this. Again it is pertinent to point out that Tagore did not want to separate Arts and Sciences but viewed them as a unified intellectual pursuit.

Second, Kala-Bhavana, which carries a huge legacy, derived from famous artists such as Nandalal, Benodbehari, Suren Kar, Ramkinkar, Somnath and more recently, Subramanyan, is still an excellent centre of art, painting and sculpture. It attracts many foreign students. What it needs today are better infrastructure, space and further globalisation. We also would want to synergise Kala-Bhavana in Santiniketan with the extant 'Shilpo-Sadana' in Sriniketan. This will allow us to strengthen the fields of design, woodcraft, etc.—a dream project of Rathindranath Tagore. The combined endeavour of Kala-Bhavana and Shilpo-Sadana can lead to a School of Design, and eventually can also grow into a School of Architecture. The ideas of National Institute of Design (NID) and Centre for Environment, Planning and Technology (CEPT) in Ahmedabad, reflect the ideologies of Visva-Bharati, but alas, we have fallen behind in living up to the expectations of the founder upacharya, Rathindranath.

A young Rabindranath Tagore

We plan to develop the vast area behind Natyaghar, all the way up to Lalbhand into an open-air theatre and park for sculptures, as a continuation of 'Kinkar Udyan' set up in the frontal portion of Malancha. In addition, the Moldanga campus in Sriniketan is being developed for a new location of Nandan Museum. For the first time in Kala-Bhavana we have started glass works in our ceramics department, which will also need facilities like furnaces, chemical etching techniques, etc.

Third, our Sangeet-Bhavana is like no other place in the world and is overflowing with immense talent. Rabindrasangeet is a serious, intellectual activity that is intertwined with history, context, creation, science, nature, and culture, and interwoven with Hindustani classical sangeet, Karnatic music, Western music, and so on. The omnipresence of 'esraj' and 'khol' has provided a unique component to Santiniketani style of Rabindrasangeet. In order to further this special school of music we have created 'Dinendra Kunja', across the road from Sangeet-Bhavana and also a Rabindrasangeet Gabeshana Kendra ('Rabi-Bitan'), to be located in 'Dakshinayan', which will carry out research in the subject, with help from colleagues drawn from Rabindra-Bhavana, other bhavanas, ashramiks and visiting scholars. We have already begun projects related to 'Kalanukramik Rabindrasangeet' and Music Board, under the auspices of 'Rabi-Bitan'.

Fourth, through projects around Rural Reconstruction, Tagore was way ahead of his time in thinking of affirmative programmes in villages adjoining Surul and Sriniketan, around the school called Siksha-Satra, and several other rural extension activities, which had pioneered community college, cooperative farming, dairy development, employment generation by harnessing natural talents of villagers in weaving, pottery, handicrafts and so on. Today we have more than 50 villages to carry this message forward. But futuristically, we want to link up education programmes in Vinay-Bhavana with rural education, especially of women, and we hope the newly appointed Director (a post which had unfortunately remained vacant for years) of Innovative Education and Rural Reconstruction to provide fillip to this activity. Once again, MHRD has recommended universities to create community colleges, but fortunately, we already have a nucleus for that, and we want to take Tagore's Sriniketan experiment to newer heights. You may recall that Tagore was the first in India to think of applying statistics to agriculture, through the help of Prasanta Chandra Mahalanobish, who had started his career in Visva-Bharati. Statistics is one area of science that we want to effectively juxtapose with agriculture, just as we would want our Economics colleagues to contribute to the extant programme in Agro-Economics.

Fifth, with the creation of the Museum of Natural History, we can resonate with Gurudev, who was deeply worried about environment, ecology—the way we treat animals—and general degradation of nature, which finds expression today in our concern for climate changes, etc. We have an ambitious project of creating a Museum of Natural History, the first of its kind in India, which will capture some of these concerns in terms of models of extinct animals like dinosaurs, and also exhibitions of Numismatics (history of coins), our own cottage industry that existed in Surul and its neighbourhood, etc. The Museum, to be established in Moldanga, will not be just a research centre, involving our faculty in history, archaeology, geography, environmental sciences and others, but will also be open to general public in terms of viewing galleries. In order to remain alive to contemporary challenges we have initiated a programme on climate studies under the aegis of the Centre for Environmental Sciences.

Sixth, by breaking the boundaries of science and making it highly interdisciplinary, we recognise that science should not be restricted to individual topics of biology, chemistry, mathematics and physics alone, but must strive to link itself with life sciences and material sciences. We want to draw from our existing faculty to encourage some of them in these cross-discipline subjects, which our teaching programme in Integrated Sciences will feed into. We have also resurrected 'Einstein-Bhavana', a concept that has remained dormant in V-B for close to twenty years. We are going to build it in Moldanga as a think-tank centre for visitors in areas such as philosophical foundation of science, cognitive science and neuro biology, quantum theory and Vedanta, the cosmos, etc., for which an already formed national advisory committee is providing us with directions. Einstein-Bhavana is visualised as an 'Aspen Centre' that will organise regular workshops and seminars and will be equipped with guest house

Udayan, Visba-Bharati

and dormitory facilities for visitors, state-of-the art library and computer centre, etc.

Seventh, by strengthening endangered Indian languages and ancient languages like Pali, Prakrit, Santhali and even Sanskrit, we have been able to have Visva-Bharati recognised by the University Grants Commission (UGC) as a nucleating centre for the preservation of these heritage languages. We want to further reinforce these Indian languages by bringing the presently fragmented faculty in Tamil, Marathi, Odiya, etc. under one umbrella. We have recently also created separate activities for comparative literature and linguistics.

All the above projects will need improvement of our infrastructure in terms of better guest house/hostel conditions, connectivity, etc. We have already started working towards achieving these goals. 'Ratan Kuthi' and 'Purbapalli' guest houses are in better shapes, and so are our student hostels. Today, we do not have to accommodate our visitors in hotels, but we need to further improve. Once the international guest house,

'Panchabati' and the apartments adjacent to the Indira Gandhi Centre for National Integration (and International Understanding) are ship-shaped, we will be able to host a larger number of international guests, scholars-in-residence (already operational) and visiting professors (also operational).

We have a long way to travel but given the support and strength of our students, faculty, 'karmis', ashramiks and alumni, we are confident that we will be able to restore at least partially, the lost glory of Visva-Bharati. The renewed interest in the physical upkeep of the campus and in welcoming international visitors will help in reviving the vision of a true international university, in Santiniketan and Sriniketan.

Ashram-Vidyalaya and a Modern University

We all know how barren the land of Birbhum was when Tagore descended in Santiniketan at the turn of the 20th century. There were hardly any trees—what existed were the 'Santiniketan Griha' and 'Chhatimtola'.

The underlying idea of starting a *vidyalaya* here, we can presume, stemmed from a deep desire of initiating a way of life that would be profoundly embedded in our Indian heritage, steeped-in the Vedic and Upanishadic value systems. Rabindranath wanted this to be located far away from Calcutta, the British capital of India, thus insulating it from the English model of education, in order to influence a new generation of Indians in a more holistic way. In a way, one can surmise, this was Gurudev's way of seeking independence when the Congress party, under the leadership of Mahatma Gandhi, was embroiled in peaceful non-cooperation with the Raj. Images of Patha-Bhavana, which grew out of the Brahamacharya school, give us an idea how idyllic Tagore wanted it to be.

In Tagore's time and thereafter, for many years, Patha-Bhavana was a fully residential school. The boys and girls stayed together, got up in the morning to joyfully express themselves in 'Baitalik' chorus, attended classes under trees in the midst of nature and ended the day, again playing, singing and dancing together. While we have pretty much the same routine today, more than 75% students are day-scholars! So, how do we retain the kind

Clockwise from Above Left: *Santiniketan Griha in earlier times; Old Singha-Sadana; Weaver at Sriniketan; Football match; Thatched huts of Patha-Bhavana; Tennis match at Ashram ground; Drill ground; Yesteryear's Gourprangan*

Old, Open Ashram Area

of emancipated and all-encompassing education that Gurudev had dreamt of, in today's society?

Let us also think of the kind of teachers and advisors Patha-Bhavana had. Leaving aside Tagore himself, who was already a great name all over the world as a highly accomplished poet, philosopher and writer, others were Brahmabandav Upadhyay, Rebachand Gyanchand Mokhijani, Manoranjan Bandyopadhyay, Jagadananda Roy, Sashibhushan Roy Chaudhury, Shivdhan Bidyarnav, Subodh Chandra Majumdar and later, Bidhusekhar Shastri—all deeply learned men with years of creative experience. They were not straight-jacketed into one or two disciplines—they could teach and advise on almost any subject under the sun. What about today's teachers? Do we think that a year of training in a B.Ed. programme, following a Bachelor's degree is good enough? In one respect we are still fortunate—while the Kendriya Vidyalayas have at least twenty-five students to one teacher, our student to teacher ratio is about thirteen to one!

By the year 1912–14 Tagore realised that the nearby village area of Surul needed another centre of learning that would be complementary to Patha-Bhavana. Thus, with 'Kuthibari' as the nucleus, Tagore's Sriniketan experiment began with the founding of 'Siksha-Satra' in 1924, a school that would help harness the natural skill of village and tribal children in pottery, leather-works, sewing, etc.

Siksha-Satra is what in today's parlance known as a 'vocational' school. Electrical maintenances and minor repair works have also been introduced in the curriculum later to make village children employable. Like Patha-Bhavana, Siksha-Satra classes are held outside so that students can imbibe rudimentary ideas of science in terms of orientation of the sun and the moon, seasonal changes, photosynthesis, basic ecology of animal behaviour, entomology of social insects, and so on, coupled with music and arts. However, unlike Patha-Bhavana, Siksha-Satra was never envisaged to be residential. Today, we have to ponder if there is any basic difference between the two schools in terms of value-based education—are the syllabi, the examination system and the method of teaching different? Are we not led to compare the board results of the two schools because that

Above Left: *Today's Patha-Bhavana;* Right: *Siksha-Satra Baitalik*
Below Left: *Old Ghantaghar;* Right: *New Ghantaghar*

has become the sole parameter of judging 'success'? Hence, if there are no fundamental differences, why should we not think of more coherence and uniformity between the two schools, why cannot we make them an integral part of what Visva-Bharati had conceived as 'Innovative Education'? Can Patha-Bhavana and Siksha-Satra be thought of the nucleus of what one perceives as a 'community college'? In all these renewed thought processes one factor assumes a very positive dimension and that is, unlike Kendriya Vidyalayas, our school system is entirely funded by us, and hence, we have flexibility in shaping them.

Even before 1924, Visva-Bharati was established as a registered body, in 1921. Visva-Bharati is a World university, though embedded in the Indian system, and that is how Tagore had envisaged it. On the other hand, it transpires that what Gurudev wanted was a university that would have its

Cheena-Bhavana

roots in its two schools of Patha-Bhavana and Siksha-Satra, but in addition have an institution of Sangeet and Kala (which was integrated under the leadership of Dinendranath Tagore) and a centre of higher research, namely Vidya-Bhavana. This was a fantastic idea; instead we went on to add all kinds of undergraduate programmes, making it a run-of-the mill university.

Vidya-Bhavana in Gurudev's concept, and until recent times, had subsumed today's Bhasha-Bhavana, the delinking of which from Vidya-Bhavana has been a thoughtless idea, in my opinion. How does one separate philosophy from say Sanskrit or Buddhist studies? Speaking of Sanskrit, Tagore was very much attuned to the Indo-European language link between Latin and Sanskrit, and hence between Sanskrit and German. It is no coincidence that great German philosophers like Goethe and Max Mueller had a deep bonding with Eastern philosophy. We all know of course that strong moorings in Eastern thoughts had propelled Gurudev towards the ancient language and culture of China. It was but natural for him to invite Tan Yun Shan to Santiniketan in 1928. And what followed was the establishment of Cheena-Bhavana in mid 1930s.

Between the Asia's first Nobel Prize in 1913 and the latest in literature in 2012 to Mo Yan, we have traversed a century of Sino-Indian kinship in culture, language and philosophy, and we must therefore encourage the newly emerging interest of Chinese institutions for closer relations with Visva-Bharati. Concomitantly, we are pleased that UGC has recognised us as the nodal centre for 'endangered' languages of India and old languages, such as Sanskrit, Santhali, Pali and Prakrit, a resurrection of which would go a long way in rejuvenating the Tagorean motto of an Indian language identity that we seem to be alarmingly moving away from in post-colonial times.

Back to 1920's, Tagore was deeply impressed by the possibilities of spreading education to villages, and that is how the schemes of 'Rural Reconstruction', 'Palli Charcha' and 'Palli Siksha' took shape. Gurudev pioneered ideas of co-operative farming and statistics-based agricultural sciences by involving giants like Leonard Elmhirst, his own son Rathindranath, Prasanta Chandra Mahalanobis, Kalimohan Ghosh, and others. All these projects were mind boggling indeed as they preceded Bidhan Roy's Haringhata experiment or Kurien's milk revolution in Anand. However, it is well to remember that the Sriniketan activities were not meant to be a part of any structured curriculum with pre-requisite degrees for enrolment—they were visualised to be a natural and flexible evolution from basic school education. Today, of course, thanks to the Ministry of Agriculture and the Indian Council of Agricultural Sciences, we are generously funded, and Palli Siksha Bhavana (PSB) and Palli Samgathana Vibhaga (PSV), are viewed as alternative options to universities like Bidhan Chandra Krishi Vidyalaya, near Kalyani.

Post Rabindranath and Rathindranath eras, a certain detrimental thing happened and that is the mental and physical alienation of Santiniketan and Sriniketan. A feeling of elitism developed, especially amongst the influential Patha-Bhavana alumni, that Sriniketan was a second-class satellite of

Old Sriniketan

New Sriniketan

Santiniketan. In my view, however, if we keep in mind the basic purpose of Tagore's education model and his deep concern about the community, Sriniketan is central to the success or demise of Visva-Bharati. We had lost a golden opportunity, in not being able to integrate Kala-Bhavana with Shilpo-Sadan, a successful symbiosis of which could have led to a great institute of design, of the likes of the National Institute of Design (NID), in Ahmedabad. Even in terms of future expansion plans, there is no alternative but to think of Mouldanga as the second Sriniketan campus. Images of old Sriniketan and how it looks at present shows very little has changed there, unlike Santiniketan, thanks to the growth of the concrete jungles in Ratan Palli, Guru Palli and Simanta Palli areas.

As long as Gurudev was alive he was the key figure—the academic, spiritual, administrative and financial head of the institution. His word was the last—he could hire and fire people; he could allot land and housing to people that he liked; there was no auditing because the institution ran on his money—some inherited, some painfully gotten by selling his wife's ornaments and the Nobel Prize money, and some from the likes of the Maharaja of Tripura, Tarak Nath Palit and so on. All that changed when he sent that impassioned plea to Gandhi: 'Visva-Bharati is like a vessel carrying the cargo of my life's best treasure and I hope it may claim special care from my countrymen for its preservation'. The net result was Visva-Bharati was declared a central university by an Act of Parliament, indeed the first central university in the year of 1951, a couple of years before the University Grants Commission (UGC) was established.

So, what changed?—A whole lot. We bartered away our financial freedom when we decided to accept public money and came under the scrutiny of the Comptroller and Auditor General (CAG), and willy-nilly we had to accept all kinds of UGC rules and regulations. One fallout of that arrangement was that school teachers, hitherto bracketed as 'Adhayapaks' with Bhavana faculty, were forced by the UGC to be treated differently in terms of salary, service conditions, retirement ages, and so on. It has taken painful years for the community to come to terms with that reality. Also, while we retain academic freedom in designing courses, methodology of teaching and modes of examination, we are forced to follow UGC guidelines in terms of requirements of NET qualification, doctoral degrees, etc. How do we square that with our core activities of Sangeet and Kala? Could one expect a Kanika Bandyopadhyay or a Ramkinkar Baij to acquire a NET qualification or a PhD degree? We have struggled hard to remove this disparity from the UGC guidelines but some still remain.

It is important to reflect on what Tagore himself had written (in Bengali) in anticipation of the transition of Visva-Bharati:

> Today I feel fatigued and tired in trying to carry on my shoulders the multitude of responsibility of the Ashram. I have borne the burden of this institution for years. It has come to a state when well-wishers have started telling me that this Ashram has grown only because of my presence. However, such dependence on one individual is fraught with the danger of survival of the institution. Many may think this Ashram is one man's property but that is fallacious. The outcome of an intense debate that followed was the creation of a constitution which is however complex and ridden with regulations.
>
> Any constitution is an impersonal, mechanical entity. But I gave my consent to the establishment of a constitution because it can help streamline the system. The general fear that personality-driven systems lack permanence is not unfounded, especially because there could be a clash of opinion with that of the successor. If there is an orchestrated system, it is more permanent. Hence I did not object to the initiation of a constitution for our Vidyalaya. I feel I should be able to carry along others who would work with me in unison. One may argue that a written constitution smacks of impersonal presence and encourages a mechanical approach. However, one should be able to positively exploit the human energy embedded in a system that is expected to work objectively and dispassionately.

Given this background of the pre and the post-UGC periods, which more or less coincided with pre and post-Rabindra/Rathindra eras, we have now come to grapple with balancing a full-blown university (and its associated issues) with the founding father's vision of flexible, open and holistic education. We must realise that a large university cannot excel in all areas—it must try to extract a few subjects in which it can be world class and unique. Though I have perhaps not been popular in articulating this view, but if you think about it hard, it is inevitable to conclude that the unique areas in which Visva-Bharati can strive to be world class are its model of education (that begins from the very beginning), rural reconstruction, both synergised in the form of what we call 'Innovative Education' that can subsume the Vinay-Bhavana programme; Kala-Bhavana (specially pursuing what is called the Santiniketan form of Art that includes the Shilpo-Sadan programme) and finally, Rabindrasangeet, Rabindranritya and Rabindranatya—there is no other place in the world that can boast of these three important attributes of Rabindranath's creativity.

It is clear that Tagore had an abiding interest in science, though he had no formal training he had an intuitive understanding of it. He did not view science as something disjointed from arts in terms of intellectual pursuit. A living testimony of Tagore's great interest in science is the wonderful book in Bengali called *Visva Parichay*, which he completed writing four years prior to his death. However, it is well to remember that modern science is based mostly on laboratory experiments, the equipment and the requisite infrastructure of which are prohibitively expensive. Do we have the wherewithal in Visva-Bharati to cope with this need and compete with other leading science institutes in India? One silver lining is our integrated science programme to which we can attract research students from high school level and expose them to borderless and interdisciplinary areas of science. It is clear that this century's science will remain in the domain of Biological and Materials Sciences, both of which require applications of basic topics of mathematics, computer science, physics and chemistry. I also feel that Visva-Bharati is just the right place to have a forum for discussing

Khoai—the region left behind by the receding Kopai river

the philosophical foundation of science in tune with the dialogues Tagore had with Albert Einstein in the year 1930. Those discussions were couched in the language of then-emerging Quantum Theory that talks about wave-particle duality, the role of observers in measurement processes, etc. These issues are deeply rooted in the Upanishadic concept of 'Atman', or the self, and its interaction with the Creator, which states that it is crucial for man to interact with the Creator through the marvel of his Creation, that is, Nature. Inspired by these thoughts, we are planning to revive an old idea of the Einstein-Bhavana which, through an active visitors' programme involving seminars, workshops, etc., will dwell on the issues of Quantum Theory and Vedanta, the cosmos, cognitive science, science and philosophy, etc.

Tagore was also highly concerned about the environment, especially the area in and around Santiniketan. The erosion of 'khoai' region would have deeply troubled him, I am sure. The institutionalised functions of 'Briksharopan', 'Halakarshan', 'Shilpotsav' and even 'Basantotsav' were designed by Tagore to make our community conscious of the need to preserve our environment. Today's climate issues have made it all the more imperative that we expand the department of Environmental Sciences into a Centre for Climate Studies as well. It is a hugely important area of interdisciplinary science that needs at the outset inputs from biology, chemistry, geography, mathematical modelling and physics.

With the preceding analysis forming a background to what we can effectively pursue in Visva-Bharati, we come to confront the basic question raised in the title of this paper: How do we reconcile or assimilate the

Above: *Halakarshan*
Below Left: *Basantotsav;* Right: *Briksharopan*

Tagore model with the present needs and realities of a large university? It may be helpful for our discourse to imagine a paradigm from the mother of all science subjects, that is, thermodynamics. In the latter we consider what is known as a 'subsystem', which is pretty much insulated from its environment. An example of such a subsystem that is familiar to all of us would be a refrigerator, which we use at home to preserve food. The air inside the refrigerator is kept at a much lower temperature than the outside by lowering the pressure with the aid of a compressor. The refrigerator doors need insulating linings to make cooling effective. However, every time we open the door to take out or insert some items the subsystem is brought into interaction with the external world that may be called a 'heat bath'. The opening of the door immediately occasions gushing of warmer air inside raising the temperature. This process is called 'equilibration'. Much in the same manner one can term the Tagore unit of a Brahmacharya Ashram (and eventual linkage with research centres) as a subsystem wherein the inculcated values were quite at variance with standard models of education. However, with the passage of time, a multifold increase of the population and the demands of our present-

Uttarayan Complex

day lifestyle, the Tagorean subsystem is continually coming under the intrusive perturbations of the environment, which is a perfect heat bath, characterised by disorder, chaos, noise, etc. Mind you, the latter three epithets, though borrowed from thermodynamics, are an apt description of the society at large. Combined with all this is the constitutional necessity of modern India to have a balance of equity with excellence, a requirement that did not exist in Gurudev's times.

Coming back to our model of the refrigerator, we all know that in order to continually offset the interaction with the surroundings we have to provide energy from outside, namely electric power in this case, that keeps the compressor running. Similarly, to sustain the Tagorean model, we need constant infusion of money-power, hitherto provided by the Ministry. But, by and by, we are told to be not over-dependent on government supply and to instead generate our own resources, which throws up a new challenge. Ironically, it is not the core activities of Patha-Bhavana, Siksha-Satra, Kala, Sangeet and Rural Programmes that can be expected to attract substantial

Today's walled campus

grant money in comparison to science and agriculture departments. Hence, we need to continuously strive to sensitise and convince the government about monetary flow for the aforesaid curricula.

We next come to the greatest source of Tagore's intellectual property, stored in the museums and archives of Rabindra-Bhavana. Undoubtedly, the Rabindra-Bhavana is the 'Jewel in the Crown' of Visva-Bharati that attracts the attention of Tagore-admirers the world over. Normally, such an institution is not an important component of a university but Visva-Bharati is no ordinary university with all its history and legacy. Isn't then there a need to dovetail Rabindra-Bhavana with the other academic programmes of Visva-Bharati? Our efforts to initiate a research scholars' programme in Rabindra-Bhavana under the umbrella of the 'Tagore Memorial Institute' (TMI) are a step in that direction.

Though we referred to the earlier model as a subsystem, it was physically an open environment. One did not have to worry about encroachments on our land. But today's world is very different in terms of its security environment—remember that we had to go through the ignominy of the theft of the Nobel medallion. How did the university react? Well, in a knee-jerk manner, in my opinion. It created a grotesque wall system that defies aesthetics and even logic, because apart from demarcating our territory (which a much less ambitious fencing would have done), it has not served any other useful purpose. On the contrary, the walls have alienated the 'Community'—after all, a university has to be an inclusive institution that helps diffuse knowledge through what should be a porous border. How does one balance the contrary needs of security with open-mindedness which is the hallmark of liberal, universal education?

I do not have answers to the many questions I have raised but I do feel these are important issues that need to be debated if we want to fulfil our great founder's dream and vision of a university 'Where the world makes a home in a single nest'.

I conclude with the English translation of an excerpt from a letter from Rabindranath to his son Rathindranath, on 18 April 1935:

> There is no real depth in the Adhyapakas of the Ashram, who are relatively young. They are unable to impart inspirational energy to the students. They lack the seriousness, dedication and simplicity of teachers like Jagadananda, Nepalbabu and Kalimohan. That is why the present lot of Adhyapakas are unable to carry out the task of institution-building. The last of the pioneers was Shastri-moshai, but alas, he is also gone. There are others from the earlier times—though they possess positive acumen they lack its practical implementation, especially in infecting young students with enthusiasm.

I hope today's young faculty will rise to the occasion and prove Gurudev wrong.

Gitanjali and the Nobel Prize

Santiniketan Seasons through Gitanjali

We have only recently celebrated the centenary of Asia's first Nobel Prize awarded to Rabindranath Tagore. Much beyond the mere act of bestowing personal glory to Tagore, the prize had significant messages and symbolism. Given that the world is divided into five continents, it is important to reflect on the fact that the prize was not just the first in Asia, but was also the first, in any subject, outside Europe and North America.

It is also pertinent to realise that the Nobel Prize went to India—a country colonised and ruled by the British Raj. Britain, or for that matter the Western world, was not keen to promote or recognise creative works of their 'natives'. In India itself, the great scientist Jagadish Chandra Bose, the discoverer of electro-magnetic communication had been denied the Nobel Prize. Satyendranath Bose, the founder of Bose-Einstein statistics based on which half the world's particles are called Bosons, named after Bose, did not receive the prize either. It is astonishing to ponder on how many Nobel Prizes in physics that have been awarded, subsequent to the establishment in 1924 of Bose-Einstein statistics—on Lasers, Bose Condensation, Coherence, and so on, and on the newly discovered Higgs Boson—owe their direct lineage to Satyendranath Bose's contribution. Meghnad Saha, the inventor of the Ionisation Formula, based on which one can measure the temperature of the Sun and other stars, is arguably the founder of modern solar physics. Yet the British establishment actively campaigned against and thereby delayed Saha's election to the Royal Society because of Meghnad's purported link with the 'Santal Dal' of East Bengal, which the British dubbed as a terrorist organisation. Last but not least, Mahatma Gandhi, who is called the 'Apostle of Peace', was not considered for the Peace Prize!

Tagore did not travel to Stockholm to receive the prize. The celebration was muted, though we have some records of felicitation by the local Bengalis and the Orient Club of Calcutta. Given this background and the fact that the British Empire had to tacitly accept the extraordinarily multifaceted talent of Rabindranath and chose not to stand in the way of the highest recognition, the actual event of the award, in 1913, did cause a stir in the Western world. Concomitantly, it triggered a resurgence, a rejuvenation of self-belief and confidence. This was ironic indeed, as it is the East that is the seat of all deep philosophies and major edicts of the world, be it the Upanishads and the Vedas, Buddhism, Islam, Hinduism, Judaism and even Christianity—remember that Jesus Christ was born in Bethlehem. Therefore, the centenary of Asia's first Nobel Prize in 2013 and the award of the Nobel Prize in literature to China's Mo Yan in 2014 are also willy-nilly a celebration of the re-incarnation of the new Asia.

The citation of the 1913 Nobel Prize in literature had centred on *Gitanjali*—Tagore's *Song Offerings*. The latter is a compendium of a few poems many of which were adorned by tunes given by Tagore, thus justifiably claiming the epithet of 'Rabindrasangeet'.

Tagore's novels, plays, and short stories bravely dealt with complex social issues and daringly challenged the extant system of then-Bengal. They are still highly relevant to present society, be it in the area of women's-emancipation, children's rights, freedom of expressions, democratic values, human dignity and so on. In contrast, the *Gitanjali* poems are more expansive and spiritual, dealing with the marvel of creation, universalism of human thoughts and the wonder of our existence itself.

In his discussion with the great German physicist Albert Einstein, Rabindranath had extolled the virtue of man and its interaction with the physical world—the two are inseparable as far as he is concerned. Here are some poems from *Gitanjali*[1] that are offerings to the Creator of this bewildering Nature, expressed through Tagore's fascination for the seasonal changes of Santiniketan. In this deep abiding love for nature we discover Rabindranath's strong spiritual affinities with the great Indian classical poet, Kalidasa.

Though the season of summer in Birbhum is scorchingly oppressive, Tagore could derive delight and happiness even in the midst of its sweltering heat. For him, despair had to be followed by hope, grief by happiness, just as night is followed by day:

> He it is, the innermost one, who awakens my being with his deep hidden touches.
> He it is who puts his enchantment upon these eyes and joyfully plays on the chords of my heart in varied cadence of pleasure and pain.
> He it is who weaves the web of this *maya* in evanescent hues of gold and silver, blue and green, and lets peep out through the folds his feet, at whose touch I forget myself.

Tagore felt the presence of the Creator through the splendour of nature, which is also reflected in his music and paintings.

> I know not how thou singest, my master! I ever listen in silent amazement.
> The light of thy music illumines the world. The life breath of thy music run from sky to sky. The holy stream of thy music breaks through all stony obstacles and rushes on.
> My heart longs to join in thy song, but vainly struggles for a voice. I would speak, but speech breaks not into song, and I cry out baffled. Ah, thou hast made my heart captive in the endless meshes of thy music, my master!

Thus when the relentless sun beats down the parched throat the thirst is suddenly quenched by the onset of a norwester:

> When the heart is hard and parched up, come upon me with a shower of mercy.
> When grace is lost from life, come with a burst of song.
> When tumultuous work raises its din on all sides shutting me out from beyond, come to me, my lord of silence, with thy peace and rest.
> When my beggarly heart sits crouched, shut up in a corner, break open the door, my king, and come with the ceremony of a king.
> When desire blinds the mind with delusion and dust, O thou holy one, thou wakeful, come with thy light and thy thunder.

Tagore resonated with the cyclic fluctuation of Birbhum seasons. He made himself a fellow-traveller with the flow of seasonal changes:

> This is my delight, thus to wait and watch at the wayside where shadow chases light and the rain comes in the wake of the summer.
> Messengers, with tidings from unknown skies, greet me and speed along the road. My heart is glad within, and the breath of the passing breeze is sweet.
> From dawn till dusk I sit here before my door, and I know that of a sudden the happy moment will arrive when I shall see.
> In the meanwhile I smile and I sing all alone. In the meanwhile the air is filling with the perfume of promise.

Rabindranath reserved his best for the monsoon or the rainy season—he wrote numerous poems and songs, very romantic ideas flowed torrentially like the floods in the Kopai river or the great Padma. Here is the Poet on his way to the favourite abode: Silaidaha.

> Clouds heap upon clouds and it darkens. Ah, love, why dost thou let me wait outside at the door all alone?
> In the busy moments of the noontide work I am with the crowd, but on this dark lonely day it is only for thee that I hope.
> If thou showest me not thy face, if thou leavest me wholly aside, I know not how I am to pass these long, rainy hours.
> I keep gazing on the far away gloom of the sky, and my heart wanders wailing with the restless wind.

The month of 'sravana', which ironically is the one of the Poet's passing, occupies a dominant space in his repertoire. Scores of emotion-soaked poems flowed from his creative pen:

> In the deep shadows of the rainy July, with secret steps, thou walkest, silent as night, eluding all watchers.
> To-day the morning has closed its eyes, heedless of the insistent calls of the loud east wind, and a thick veil has been drawn over the ever-wakeful blue sky.
> The woodlands have hushed their songs, and doors are all shut at every house. Thou art the solitary wayfarer in this deserted street. Oh my only friend, my best beloved, the gates are open in my house—do not pass by like a dream.

Or, even more passion-filled:

> Art thou abroad on this stormy night on thy journey of love, my friend? The sky groans like one in despair.
> I have no sleep to-night. Ever and again I open my door and look out on the darkness, my friend!
> I can see nothing before me. I wonder where lies thy path lies!
> By what dim shore of the ink-black river, by what far edge of the frowning forest, through what mazy depth of gloom art thou threading thy course to come to me, my friend?

Rabindranath Tagore on the banks of Padma with Shilaidaha subjects

In autumn the Santiniketan sky acquires a distinctive hue of clear blue, providing a contrasting balance with the wheatish jungle of 'kash' flowers, on the ground.

> Yes, I know, this is nothing but thy love, O beloved of my heart—this golden light that dances upon the leaves, these idle clouds sailing across the sky, this passing breeze leaving its coolness upon my forehead.
> The morning light has flooded my eyes—this is thy message to my heart. Thy face is bent from above, thy eyes look down on my eyes, and my heart has touched thy feet.

Well, autumn and winter pass by, but the season that can compete with the rains for capturing the outburst of Tagore's emotions is none other than the spring. Gurudev immortalised love that accompanies the spring air by composing for *Gitanjali*:

> He came and sat by my side but I woke not. What a cursed sleep it was, O miserable me!
> He came when the night was still; he had his harp in his hands, and my dreams became resonant with its melodies.
> Alas, why are my nights all thus lost? Ah, why do I ever miss his sight whose breath touches my sleep?

Finally, an example of rejoicing the spectacular radiance of light, which blesses our Mother Earth, from the sun, the moon, the stars—light that nourishes plants and creates oxygen, the source of life:

> Light, my light, the world-filling light, the eye-kissing light, heart-sweetening light!
> Ah, the light dances, my darling, at the centre of my life; the light strikes, my darling, the chords of my love; the sky opens, the wind runs wild, laughter passes over the earth.
> The butterflies spread their sails on the sea of light. Lilies and jasmines surge up on the crest of the waves of light.
> The light is shattered into gold on every cloud, my darling, and it scatters gems in profusion.
> Mirth spreads from leaf to leaf, my darling, and gladness without measure. The heaven's river has drowned its banks and the flood of joy is abroad.

Endnote

1. *Gitanjali: Song Offerings*, by Rabindranath Tagore, Rabindra-Bhavana, Visva-Bharati, 2013

Song Offerings, 1912

Song Offerings, written in 1912, comprise English translations of original Bengali verses that had earlier appeared in *Gitanjali, Gitimalya, Naibadya, Kheya* and other Bengali writings of the Poet. It is indeed *Song Offerings* that constitute the citation of the 1913 Nobel Prize in Literature, Asia's first in any subject.

Tagore wrote extensively and almost exclusively in Bengali. Why did he then venture into writing in English? Was that a sudden, impulsive decision or was there a method in it? We have found no evidence to suggest any conscious planning behind the composition of *Song Offerings*. It appears to be a random wish on Tagore's part to try his hand at English, perhaps accentuated by the sea-voyage, full of expectations that would take him from the shore of India to that of England, in May 1912.[1]

It is also common knowledge that Rabindranath travelled extensively in the 1920s to Europe, the Americas, and Asian nations, in particular China, Japan, Sri Lanka and Iran. He abhorred nationalism—indeed he was international in his outlook. Therefore, it was but perhaps natural that he would want to translate his writings into English, in order to make them accessible to a wider audience, English being already an accepted international mode of communication. Besides, Tagore was often vilified by his own countrymen and he found solace from a more appreciative Western audience.

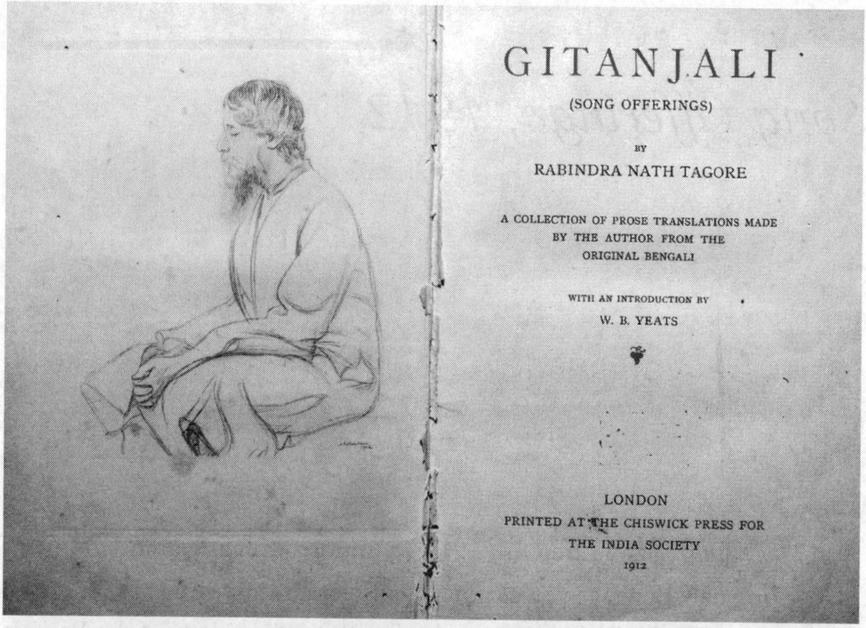

GITANJALI

(SONG OFFERINGS)

BY

RABINDRA NATH TAGORE

A COLLECTION OF PROSE TRANSLATIONS MADE
BY THE AUTHOR FROM THE
ORIGINAL BENGALI

WITH AN INTRODUCTION BY

W. B. YEATS

LONDON
PRINTED AT THE CHISWICK PRESS FOR
THE INDIA SOCIETY
1912

ABOVE: *First page of* Song Offerings
BELOW: *J.C. Bose and others greeting the Bard in 1913 in Santiniketan*

Nobel Medallion

In support of this assessment we translate from 'Alap-Alochana' between Rabindranath Tagore and Dilip Kumar Roy, in *Sangitchinta*[2]:

> I was impulsively putting into English some of the verses of *Gitanjali*. Basically, I had nothing else to do as I was down in bed with illness. I could not dare to think even in my wildest dreams to get the English versions published. The reason is, I had firmly believed that I was incapable of writing in English which was worthy of publication.
>
> When my *Gitanjali* translations landed in the hands of Yeats he decided to invite a bunch of English writers and connoisseurs to Rothenstein's home to read aloud the poems. I was naturally embarrassed, because of two reasons: First I could never satisfy Bengalee listeners, within ten to twelve lines of poetry, which they considered inadequate. They even attributed the compactness of the poems to my deficiency. Many of them would even regret that I was devoting most of my time to writing songs. They saw in this the onset of the new-moon time when, like the size of the moon, my poetry was also getting shrunk in size. Second, I had shown my English

Rabindranath Tagore with Rothenstein

translations with some trepidation to knowledgeable Bengalis. They had quite condescendingly proclaimed that my effort was not bad and that the English was not incorrect! At that time I was not acquainted with C.F. Andrews whom I could have used as a bouncing board.

In that gathering in the Rothenstein home, Yeats read out just five to seven poems. The British listeners heard quietly and left quietly, without the customary exchange of greetings. I returned home that night with a feeling of being small. The next day however, I saw a flurry of appreciative mails—I was totally overwhelmed by the unexpected recognition that I received from a distant land.

In this context it is interesting to analyse the Bard's views on music, in general, and Indian music vis-à-vis Western music, mostly articulated in the decade of 1920. He professes to Einstein in 1930:

> It is difficult to analyze the effect of eastern and western music on our minds. I am deeply moved by the western music—I feel that it is great, that it is vast in its structure and grand in comparison. But our music touches me more deeply by its fundamental lyrical appeal.

To this, Albert Einstein asks, 'When did you first hear European music?' Tagore answers:

> At seventeen when I first came to Europe, but even before that in my household, I had heard the music of Chopin and others at an early age.

To Rolland (in 1926) he had earlier said:

> I have always felt the immense power of European music. I love Beethoven and also Bach.

Yet seventeen long years after receiving the highest accolade from the Swedish Academy, the Poet asks H.G. Wells in 1930[3]:

> I have composed more than 300 pieces of music. They are all sealed to the West because they cannot properly be given to you in your own notation. They would not perhaps be intelligible to your people even if I could get them written down in European notation.

To this, Wells remarks optimistically: 'The West may get used to the music.'

But, why do we talk about music when our focus has been on *Gitanjali* and *Song Offerings*, which contain verses? Well, the answer lies in the very name *Gitanjali*. 'Geet' in Bengali is music, which became the chosen form of the title rather than say, 'Kabyanjali'. For Tagore, verse and music are one and the same—both are lyrics and therefore, behind the creation of *Gitanjali* and *Song Offerings*, we discover Tagore, the lyricist.

It is pertinent now to recall what Tagore comments to Marguerite Wilkinson in an interview in Indian Poetry, in 1921:

> Our people love to chant poetry. I know villagers in my neighbourhood, who after their day's work in the field, gather under the stars before some hut and sing in chorus till midnight devotional songs belonging to the best lyrical literature of their language.

Wilkinson further asks, 'If the people enjoy singing your poem is it because they are like folk poetry?' to which Tagore says:

> Some of my poems are like folk poetry but some are in the romantic style and some in the classical style.

A question naturally arises: When Tagore was involved in translating his verses into English, was he thinking of the West's acceptability of Indian music and also, was he aware of the pitfalls of translation? The answer to both these queries is 'Yes'. In a dialogue with Edward Thompson in 1926, fourteen years after he wrote *Song Offerings*, Gurudev remarked:

> It is nonsense to say that music is a universal language—I know this cannot be, unless not till the West has had time to study and learn to appreciate our music.

About translations, he commented to Rolland, also in 1926, that:

> In poetry, a particular work possesses a subtle atmosphere of its own literary associations. The peculiar value of such words will never be intelligible to foreigners; they cannot be appreciated as being supremely beautiful by merely listening to them, or even by merely understanding their literal meaning, for the association will be lacking.

In support of this point of view, Tagore quoted from Keats:

> '[M]agic casement opening on the foam of perilous seas in faery lands forlorn.' If I translate it into Bengali, it will become meaningless.

Song Offerings include a total of 103 verses, most of which relate to Tagore's spiritual leanings on Upanishada and his obeisance to the Almighty, the Creator, hence the phrase 'anjali' or 'offerings', that suffixes the title. On the other hand, the Bengali *Gitanjali* contains many verses (and their song renditions) about the rainy season.

Most of these verses on *varsha* are based on Raga Malhar of classical music but have tinges of many other ragas, but the point is—and it is an essential point—that it is futile to seek any specific 'raga' behind Tagore's music. In *Sangitchinta* he writes to Indira Devi, which in English reads:

> It is undesirable to ordain musical notes with rules, directions, etc. because any kind of regimentation opens room for scrutiny and does not conform to aesthetics. It is not necessary to spell out what 'raga' a particular song is based on—what is important is how it is sung, because that brings out the core honesty of a song. Rules bind people who however may disagree on the modes of expression.

The following quote from Tagore's 'Alap-Alochana' with Dilip Kumar Roy further amplifies this point:

> Why do you not recognise that there is a fundamental difference between Hindustani music and the one I have created? Why do you not admit that classical tunes manifest themselves as liberated minds, but do not want to have lyrics as partners? On the other hand, songs of Bengal do not believe in celibacy but are in quest for cohabitation with words. Melody and lyric, in the context of Bengal, are

naturally synergised—they flourish in complementary form of coexistence. It is like in a marriage, in which though the man apparently assumes a position of dominance, it is futile to further fragment the unit that the couple forms to discern which partner is more important. Thus, Bengal's music is like a wedded family in which melody and lyric are bonded together—it is not prudent to see them disjointedly. The situation in the case of Hindustani music is quite different—it is not affected if words are given short shrift and the performer simply adjusts the tune in the form of 'Ta-Na-Na', devoid of any poetic meaning.

As I am not claiming that Bengal's songs, especially the modern ones, are not rooted in Hindustani origin, you (meaning D.L. Roy) are free to give my form of music any other appellation—I have no objection. A large banyan tree is noted for its extravagant spread of its trunks and branches, but a palm tree is distinguished for the sparsity of leaves. Do not compare a palm tree with a banyan tree. In fact, a palm tree would begin to look ugly if it were to be given the appearance of a banyan tree! Its beauty is in fact in its simplicity of form. If you do not like it, you can take refuge under the banyan tree—for me, both are nice, and hence my chosen path is sought to embrace the palm tree as self as the banyan tree. But if you want to rejoice by supplanting the trunks and branches of a banyan tree on to the torso of a palm tree, you are bound to incur the wrath of the palm grove-admirers!

Tagore further mentions to Rolland in 1926:

> Take the Indian rain songs. They do not try to imitate the sound of falling raindrops. They re-kindle the joy of rain festivals and convey something of the feeling associated with the rainy season.

It is now useful to reflect once again on the Tagore-Einstein dialogue of 1930:

AE: Can the Indian music be sung without words? Can one understand a song without words?
RNT: Yes we have songs with unmeaning words—sounds which just help to act as carriers of the notes, such as in North India, music is an independent art, not the interpretation of words and thoughts, as in Bengali. In contradistinction to rain songs, in which there are signatures of classical ragas, the verses in both *Gitanjali*, and *Song Offerings* that connote to 'sharatkal' or autumn, are rich in melody, embedded in Kirtan and Baul music.

It is interesting again to reminisce the Tagore-Einstein conversation:

RNT: There is in human affairs an element of elasticity—some freedom within a small range which is for the expression of our personality. It is like the musical system in India which is not so rigidly fixed as is the western music. Our composers give a certain definite outline, a system of melody and rhythmic arrangement, and within a certain limit the player can improvise upon it …
AE: Are the words also free? I mean to say, is the singer at liberty to add his own words to the melody which he is singing?
RNT: Yes. In Bengal we have a kind of song—'kirtan' we call it—which gives freedom to the singer to introduce parenthetical comments—known as 'aaankhor', in Bengali. These are phrases, not present in the original song. This occasions great enthusiasm, since the audience is constantly thrilled by some beautiful, spontaneous sentiment, added by the singer.

Tagore, in *Talks in China* (1925), muses:

In regard to music, I claim to be something of a musician myself, I have composed many songs which have defied the canons of orthodox propriety and good people are disgusted

> at the impudence of a man who is audacious only because he is untrained. But I persist, and God forgives me because I do not know what I do. Possibly that is the best way of doing things in the sphere of art. For I find that people blame, but also sing my songs, even if not always correctly.
>
> Please do not think I am vain. I can judge myself objectively and can openly express admiration for my own work, because I am modest. I do not hesitate to say that my songs have found their place in the heart of my land, along with her flowers that are never exhausted, and that the folk of the future, in days of joy or sorrow or festival, will have to sing them. This too is the work of a revolutionist.

Shortly thereafter, he mentions to Edward Thompson, in 1926:

> I have introduced some new element in our music, I know. I have composed five hundred new tunes, perhaps more. This is a parallel growth to my poetry. Anyhow, I love this aspect of my activity. I get lost in my songs, and then I think that these are my best work; I get quite intoxicated. I often feel that, if all my poetry is forgotten, my songs will live with my countrymen, and have a permanent place. I have very deep delight in them…All the same, I know the artistic value of my songs. They have great beauty. Though they will not be known outside my province, and much of my work will be gradually lost, I leave them as a legacy. My own countrymen do not understand but they will. They are real songs, songs for all seasons and occasions. In my hymns, my *Brahma-Sangeet,* I have adapted and taken wholesale older tunes from Tansen, the best of our composers; in these, I have used orthodox forms. But for my own songs I have invented very freely.

In these *Brahma Sangeet* or Upasana-songs, many of which also feature in the 'Puja' edition of *Gitanjali*, Tagore advances his argument on behalf of

Quantum Theory that he made to Einstein. This concerns the ubiquitous role of the 'observer' in what is being 'observed'. Unless the self or 'Aham' or 'Atman' interacts with the Almighty, or the other way round, how can the marvel of creation be appreciated by Man? Or, even more daringly, Tagore opines:

> It is in the interest of the Creator that he descends to a level in which He can interact with man in order to unravel the splendour of creation.

We once again return to the basic theme of 'lyrics' that capture the ethos and pathos of Tagore. In her interview in 1921, cited earlier, Marguerite Wilkinson asks: 'When you make a poem and music for it do you make the verbal and musical melodies together? Or, does the music come first, so that you fit words to it, or the words, so that you fit music to them?' Tagore answers:

> Sometimes I make the words first and then put music with them later. Sometimes I make a melody first and then put words to it. Sometimes the music is subordinated to the words; sometimes the words are subordinated to music.

Wilkinson is bemused: 'How does this method affect your rhythms?' Tagore replies:

> They are always changed. Anything new added always changes what was before. It is like colour added to the lines of a picture. When you put melody to words the rhythm is changed.

This unique approach of Tagore to the composition of his music is further elaborated in the dialogue with Einstein when the latter comments: 'Sometimes melody in western music suffers much as harmony swallows up the melody altogether.' Gurudev reiterates what he had told Wilkinson earlier:

> Melody and harmony[1] are like lines and colours in pictures. A simple linear picture may be completely beautiful; the introduction of colour may make it vague and insignificant. Yet colour may, by combination with lines, create great pictures so long as it does not smother and destroy their value.

Einstein was deeply impressed: 'It is a beautiful comparison; line is also much older than colour. It seems your melody is much richer in structure than ours.'

In this context what Gurudev mentions to Dilip Kumar Roy in 'Alap-Alochana' is also worth mentioning. Here is a translation:

> There is duality in every creation—its one side is the internal truth while the other side is the external carrier. That is, one side constitutes the feeling while the other is expressed through words. Both are organically linked but are characteristically distinct. The words are not universal as the inner truth is. In order to understand it one must comprehend the outer encasement. For instance, one must master the language of English in order to relish the juice of Shelley's poetry—it is not possible to separate the intimate link between the language and the associated emotion.
>
> The inner core of music is international but its outer coating is nation-specific. If the container is not properly dealt with, the food inside loses its delicacy. But then, it will be erroneous to doubt the quality of the food. I have witnessed how seriously and deeply the Europeans view their music—it will be foolhardy for me not to appreciate or admire it—but I am unable to penetrate within, as I lack the facility of their language.

In conclusion, it is significant to ponder on the fact that it is between 1907 and 1912 that Tagore had reached the pinnacle of his unfathomable creativity. The year 1907 also marks a watershed in his life when Tagore got a bit disillusioned with the nationalistic movement, which came in the wake of the agitation against the partition of Bengal. He could never think of himself as constrained by the boundaries of a nation—his empathy lied with 'Manab' or 'Human', irrespective of country, caste, creed, religion, etc. That is why we surmise that Tagore chose to undertake numerous foreign trips in the twenties, though in frail health. Indeed, we know of no other contemporary Indian who had made so many sojourns abroad and had interacted with so many common people, in addition to a galaxy of great thinkers: Einstein, Rolland, Bernard Shaw, Sigmund Freud, Helen Keller, Yeats, Rothenstein, Victoria Ocampo and others. Here we discover a *universal* Tagore whose lifelong motto was to seek East-West harmony.

All the quotes in this article have been taken from Rabindranath Tagore's *Jibansmriti* and *Sangitchinta*. It may be underscored here that *Sangitchinta* is actually an anthology or compilation that constitutes a collection of various music-related articles of Rabindranath. This was published by the Visva-Bharati Music Board in the form of a book, twenty-five years after the Poet's passing.

Endnotes

1. Besides *Song Offerings* Tagore had also written, during this aforesaid sea-voyage, essays like 'Antar-Bahir', 'Sangeet', etc. These were compiled in *Pather Sanchay* way before *Sangitchinta* was published.
2. Note that Tagore's conversation with Dilip Kumar Roy and Indira Devi were in Bengali, unlike with Rolland, Einstein, Wells.
3. It is interesting to note that the number mentioned by Tagore to Wells is only 300, though in point of fact, he had composed by 1930, more than 1000 pieces of music. We surmise that Gurudev perhaps had given only a selective account of those compositions that capture the synergy between melody and rhythm, which Tagore considered to be the hallmark of western music.
4. Here Tagore implies both words and instruments.

Tagore Across Cultures: The Nobel Prize and Beyond

Alfred Nobel had willed the Nobel Prize for Literature for 'the most outstanding work in an ideal direction'. The Swedish Academy interpreted 'ideal' as 'idealistic'. Tagore's writings apparently fitted-in with this requirement but it is significant to recognise that giant authors like Ibsen and Tolstoy were never awarded the prize because they were thought to be not romantic enough! Although Tagore's works did qualify, it is interesting to point out that few of the Swedish decision-makers on the Nobel Committee had read *Song Offerings*—they were impressed by the persuasive powers of the Irish poet, Yeats.

So how did Tagore take the prize? It is well known that Rabindranath was an extremely reticent person, almost shy of publicity or personal glorification. In a telegram to Rothenstein, in whose home selected verses of *Song Offerings* had been read out by Yeats to a few English poets (in 1912), Tagore wrote in November 1913:

> I am being smothered with telegrams and letters for the last few days and the people who never read a line of my works are loudest in their protestations of joy.

Eight years later, in July 1921, Tagore relates his feeling to C.F. Andrews:

William Butler Yeats

It is far better for a poet to miss his reward in this life than to have a false reward or to have it in excessive measure. The man who constantly received honour from admiring crowds has the grave danger of developing a habit of mental parasitism upon such honour—he consciously or unconsciously grows to crave for it and feels injured when his allowance is curtailed or withdrawn. I feel frightened of such possibility in me—for it is vulgar. Unfortunately when a person has some mission of doing some kind of public good, his popularity becomes the best asset for him—his own people readily follow him when other people have the same readiness—and this makes it a matter of temptation for such an individual. My International University is sure to create such a risk for me. And yet fulfilment of my

> life is never in any ambitious scheme like this. And therefore a voice of warning is constantly troubling me in my heart, it cries: 'Poet, fly away to your solitude'. Further, in an undated letter to Andrews, he writes: 'One day I shall have to fight my way out of my own reputation—for the call of my Padma still comes to me through this huge and growing barrier. It says—'Poet, where are you?' and all my heart and soul try to seek out that poet. It has been difficult to find him—for the great multitude of men have heaped honours on him—and he cannot be extricated from under them.

It is pertinent to reflect on what the Poet himself thought of the West's appreciation of the so-called 'Indian Identity' that pervades through the deep philosophical basis of the verses of *Song Offerings*. On this, he writes in 'Creative Unity':

> The bringing about of an intellectual unity in India is, I am told, difficult to the verge of impossibility owing to the fact that India has so many different languages. Such a statement is as unreasonable as to say that man, because he has a diversity of limbs should find it impossible to realise life's unity, and that only an earthworm composed of tail and nothing else could truly know that it had a body.

However, the dichotomy in Gurudev's mind, yielding a lifelong pre-occupation with duality of the East and the West, led him to write in 'Creative Unity':

> Let me say that I have no distrust of any culture because of its foreign character. On the contrary, I believe that the shock of such extraneous forces is necessary for the vitality of our intellectual nature… the European culture has come to us, not only with its knowledge, but with its velocity.

On West's strength in pursuing scientific thoughts, he adds:

> Let us admit that modern science is Europe's great gift to humanity for all time to come. We, in India, must claim it from her hands, and gratefully accept it to be saved from the curse of futility by lagging behind. We shall fail to reap the harvest of the present age if we delay.

He writes to Andrews in Oct 1913:

> In India the range of our lives is narrow and discontinuous, that is the reason why our minds are beset with provincialism.

And again in July 1920:

> When I am in the West I feel more strongly than ever that I am received in a living world of mind. I miss here my sky and light and leisure, but I am in touch with those who feel and express their need of me and whom I can offer myself. Our span of life is short and opportunity rare, so let us sow our seeds of thought where the soil claims them, where the harvest will ripen.

The founding of Visva-Bharati in 1921 emanated from this idea of India—a university that would blend the vision of the East with the scientifically progressive mind of the West in order to enlighten new vistas for humanity. It is up to us in Visva-Bharati to live up to that great legacy, established by Asia's first Laureate Poet.

Tagore on National and International Relations

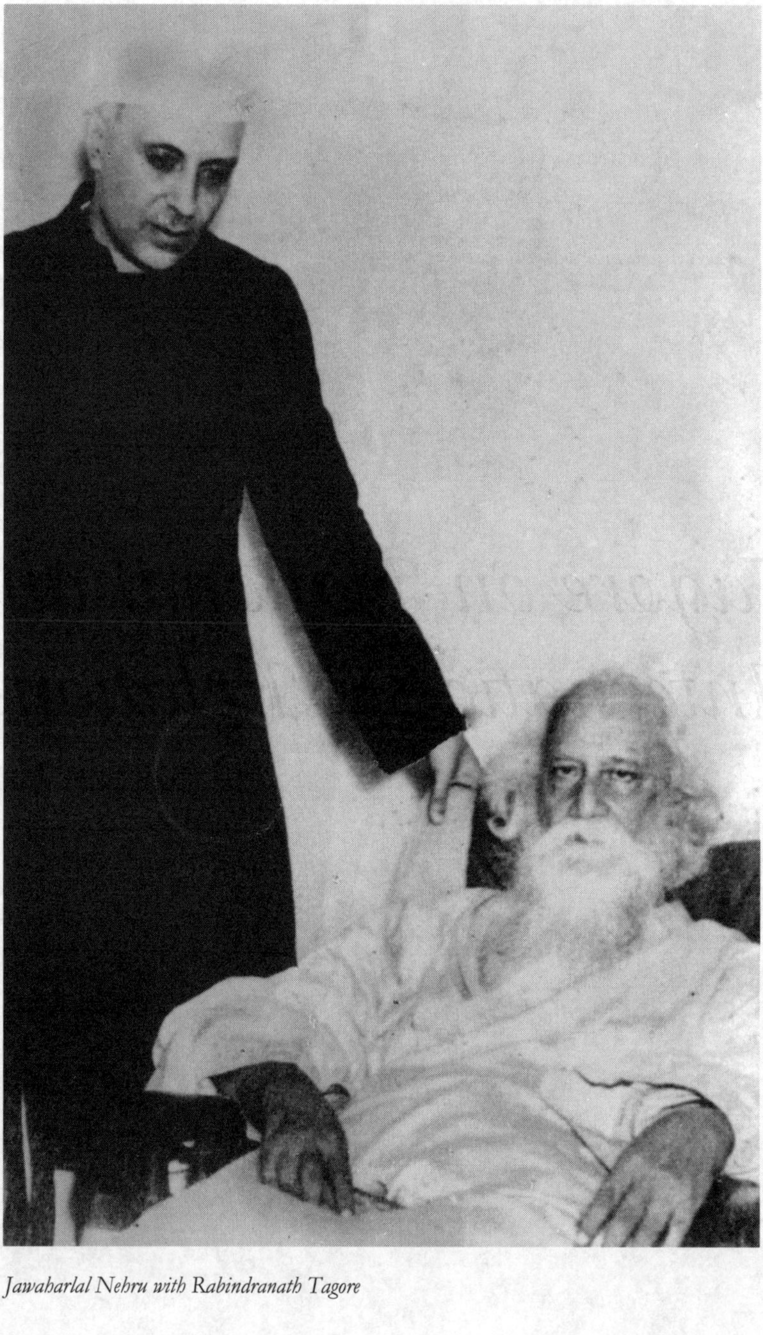

Jawaharlal Nehru with Rabindranath Tagore

Nehru, Tagore and Visva-Bharati

I once heard the noted historian and social scientist Ramachandra Guha remark that four individuals who had shaped the concept of India as a nation in the 20th century were Gandhi, Ambedkar, Nehru and Tagore. To this, a bewildered natural scientist got up to ask Guha how Tagore was included in a list of three giants of India's freedom struggle and nationalistic movement. Ram's answer was that it was the moral and spiritual voice of Tagore that gave shape to what he called the 'Indian Identity'. It is his towering voice that at least the two stalwarts of the Congress movement had to come and listen to, over and again. Thus, through several visits to Santiniketan, Gandhi and Nehru helped themselves in shaping their own political ideas of India as a nation.

What is this 'Indian Identity' that Tagore was obsessed with? Earlier in the chapter on 'Tagore Across Cultures—The Nobel Prize and Beyond' I have quoted him from 'Creative Unity':

> The bringing about of an intellectual unity in India is, I am told, difficult to the verge of impossibility owing to the fact that India has so many different languages. Such a statement is as unreasonable as to say that man, because he has a diversity of limbs should find it impossible to realise life's unity, and that only an earthworm composed of tail and nothing else could truly know that it had a body.

In contrast to Gandhi, and more in tune with Nehru who had defined 'scientific temper', Tagore embraced Western science and forms of knowledge. What he lamented, however, was the perceived imbalance between the vitality of Western knowledge with this cultivation of 'sympathy', which is at the heart of India's or, more generally, the East's ethos. On his disagreement with Gandhi's nationalistic and non-cooperation movement that repudiated the East-West harmony he wrote an anguished letter to Andrews, on 23 September 1925:

> Personally I do not think my overcautious doctor was wise in holding me back. He does not fully realise how great is the mental strain that my stay in India imposes upon me. It is the moral loneliness which is a constant and invisible burden that oppresses me most. I wish it were possible for me to join hands with Mahatma Gandhi and thus at once surrender myself to the current of popular approbation. But I can no longer hide it from myself that we are radically different in our apprehension and pursuit of truth. Today to disagree with Mahatma and yet find rest in one's surroundings in India is not possible and therefore I am waiting for my escape next March with an impatient feeling of longing. I know I have friends in Europe who are my real kindred and whose sympathy will act as a true restorative in my present state of weariness.

Yet, Tagore's writings in 'Creative Unity' on the confluence of the Vedic, the Puranic, the Buddhist and the Jain, almost echo Nehru's own *Discovery of India*:

> The main river in the Indian culture has its source in the heights of the Indian consciousness. But a river, belonging to a country, is not fed by its own waters alone....The Muhammedan, for example, has repeatedly come into India from outside, laden with his own stores of knowledge and feeling and his wonderful religious democracy, bringing freshet after freshet to swell the current.

> To our music, our architecture, our pictorial art, our literature, the Muhammadans have made their permanent and pernicious contribution. Those who have studied the lives and writings of our medieval saints, and all the great religious movements that sprang up in the time of the Muhammadan rule, know how deep is our debt to this foreign current that has so intimately mingled with our life. Along with that came three other strains—the eastern idea, flowing from China and Japan and from the western borders of India—the Sikh and the Zoroastrian.

He wrote to C.F. Andrews in April 1921:

> From the beginning of their history the western races have had to deal with nature as their antagonist. This fact has emphasised in their mind the dualistic aspect of truth, the eternal conflict between good and evil. Thus West has kept up the spirit of fight in the heart of their civilisation. They seek victory and cultivate power.
>
> The environment in which the Aryan immigrants found themselves in India was that of the forest. The forest, unlike the desert or rock or sea, is living, it gives shelter and nourishment to life. In such a surrounding the ancient forest dwellers of India realised the spirit of harmony with the universe, and emphasised in their mind the monastic aspect of truth. They sought the realisation of their soul through the union with all. The spirit of fight and the spirit of harmony, both have their importance in the scheme of things. For making a musical instrument, the obduracy of materials has to be forced to yield to the purpose of the instrument-maker. But music itself is a revelation of beauty, it is not an outcome of fight; it springs from an inner realisation of harmony. The musical instrument and music both have their utmost importance for humanity. The civilisation that conquers for man, and the civilisation that realises for him the fundamental unity in the depth of existence, are complementary

> to each other. When they join hands human nature finds its balance and its pursuits through their rugged paths attain their ultimate meaning in an ideal of perfection.

In 'Creative Unity' Tagore once again bemoans the Eastern attempt to embrace the Western cult of power and adulation of money:

> The whole of the human world, throughout its length and breadth, has felt the gravitational pull of a giant planet of greed, with concentric rings of innumerable satellites, causing in our society a marked deviation from the moral orbit.

And:

> Once upon a time we were in possession of such a thing as our own mind in India. It was living. It thought, it felt, it expressed itself. The wholesale acceptance of modern, western education has suppressed this mind. It has been treated like a wooden library shelf to be loaded with volumes of second-hand information; in consequence, it has lost its own colour and character, and has borrowed polish from the carpenter's shop…we have bought our spectacles at the expense of our eyesight.

Furthermore:

> If we were to take it for granted, what some people maintain, that western culture is the only source of light for our mind, then it would be like depending for daybreak upon some star, which is the sun of a far distance sphere. The star may give us light, but not the day; it may give us direction in our voyage of exploration, but it can never open the full view of much before our eyes. In fact, we can never use this cold starlight for stirring the sap in our branches, and giving colour and bloom to our life.

In the wake of the Jalianwala Bag massacre, which made him return the Knighthood, Tagore was however prompted to write to C.F. Andrews on 9 September 1920:

> Stung by insult and injustice, we try to repudiate Europe, but by doing it we insult ourselves. Let us have the dignity not to quarrel or retaliate, not to pay back in smallness with being small ourselves. What Gandhi is inculcating in his pugnacious spirit of resentment is the withdrawal of service from the government. It is a wasteful diversion of the best part of our energy to a course which ends in mere emptiness of negation. This is the time when we should dedicate all our resources of emotion, thought and character to the service of our country in a positive direction….
>
> … [T]he moral fervour which the life of Gandhi represents and which he, of all other men in the world, can call up, is needed. That such a precious treasure of power should be put into the mean and frail vessel of our politics allowing it to sail across endless waves of angry recrimination is terribly unfortunate for our country where our mission is to revive the dead with the fire of soul…it is not that I do not feel anger in my heart for injustice and insult heaped upon my motherland. But this anger of mine should be turned into the fire of love…India can live and grow by spreading abroad, not the political India, but the ideal India. Our Santiniketan is for this mission. We must fully know this ideal India and then will come the time when we shall be able to carry her abroad and once again her history will find fulfilment in the present age.

It is this common ideal of giving shape to the East-West harmony in the form of Visva-Bharati that brought Nehru close to Tagore: What was Nehru's position in this extraordinary triangle, of the three most remarkable individuals in Indian history who formed the other two vertices of the triangle? To quote Jawaharlal himself:

> … My mind was a little more in tune with Tagore although all my activities were conditioned by Gandhiji.

He further amplifies:

> … [T]he more I have read what Tagore wrote about 'Some aspects of the new movement Gandhi had started', the more I have appreciated it and felt, in tune with it. Tagore's article: 'The Call of Truth' and Gandhi's reply: 'The Great Sentinel' were wonderful reading then and I should say, even now. They represented two aspects of the truth, neither of which could be ignored.

And again, 'In later years', Nehru stresses:

> … [M]y attraction to Tagore grew. I felt a great deal of kinship with his thought and with his general outlook in life. I visited him in Santiniketan on several occasions, during the intervals of my life outside the prison.

Nehru emphasises that Tagore and Gandhi—

> … [S]eemed to present different but harmonious aspects of India and to complement each other.

What did Tagore himself think of Nehru?

> … Jawaharlal has his undoubted right to the throne of Young India. His is a majestic character—unflinching in his patient determination and indomitable in his courage. But what raises him far above his fellows is his unwavering adherence to moral integrity and intellectual honesty. He has kept unusually high the standard of purity in the midst of political turmoil, where deceptions of all kinds, including that of one's self, runs rampant.

> He has never fought shy of truth where it was dangerous—nor made allowance with falsehood when it would be convenient. His brilliant intellect has ever turned away in outspoken disgust from the dishonourable path of policies where success is as easy as it is mean. This lofty ideal of truth is Jawaharlal's greatest contribution in his fight for freedom.

On the other hand, so impressed was Nehru with the Tagore model of holistic and universal education that he put his only child under Tagore's care, about which he writes:

> I sent my daughter Indira to Santiniketan hoping that she would imbibe something of the atmosphere of the place and, more particularly, profit it by the presence of and contact with Gurudev.

He regretted that Indira had to be withdrawn midway so that she could accompany her ailing mother Kamala to Switzerland in the absence of her imprisoned father. About this, Nehru wrote to Tagore in April 1935:

> … She has to cut short her career at Santiniketan and I am exceedingly sorry that she should have to do so. I have seen very little of her during her year at Santiniketan—the last time I had a brief glimpse of her at a gaol interview was nearly six months ago. But even these brief glimpses, as well as the reports I have had from friends, have convinced me how well she was getting on there. Her own testimony and that is important enough, is clear and she has been very happy at Santiniketan and has no desire whatever to leave it. I was looking forward to her remaining there for a longer period and growing in mind and body under your sheltering care and guidance. It was a great consolation for me in prison that my daughter was surrounded by loving and capable friends who were gently helping in her development in

> the right direction, and I felt infinitely grateful to all of them for the love and kindness they showered on her. I rejoiced that I had been fortunate enough to choose Santiniketan for her education at this stage of her life.

The Poet responded four days later:

> It is with a heavy heart we bade farewell to Indira, for she was such an asset in our place. I have watched her very closely and have felt admiration for the way you have brought her up. Her teachers, all in one voice, praise her and I know she is extremely popular with the students. I only hope things will turn for the better and she will soon return here and get back to her studies.

Tagore chose Jawaharlal for the inauguration of the Cheena-Bhavana, for both Tagore and Nehru were in unison in their belief that China and India were critically important for the rejuvenation of Asia. Nehru could not be present but his inaugural address was read out on 14 April 1937 by her daughter Indira. Later Nehru did indeed make it to the opening of the Hindi-Bhavana in January 1939.

The discussion on these two great Indians would be incomplete if we do not mention what Nehru had to say about the 'Jana Gana Mana' written by Tagore:

> During my last visit to him I requested him to compose a national anthem for the New India. He partly agreed. At that time I did not have 'Jana Gana Mana'—our present National Anthem in mind. He died soon after. It was a great happiness to me when some years later after the coming of independence, we adopted 'Jana Gana Mana' as our National Anthem. I have a feeling of satisfaction that I was partly responsible for this choice, not only because it is a great national song, but also because it is a constant reminder to all our people of Rabindranath Tagore.

Nehru heard the news of Tagore's passing on 7 August 1941 from the Dehradun jail. He wrote to Krishna Kripalini, on 27 August 1941:

> How long ago it all seems! People must die some time or other and Gurudeva could not have lived much longer. And yet his death came as a grievous shock to me and the thought that I would never see his beautiful face and hear his gentle voice again oppressed me terribly. Ever since I came to prison this thought had haunted me. I wanted to see him once again so much. Not that I had anything special to say to him, and certainly I had no desire to trouble him in any way. Perhaps the premonitions that I was not fated to see him again itself added to this yearning.
>
> However, all that is over and, instead of sorrow, let us rather congratulate ourselves that we were privileged to come in contact with this great and magnificent person. Perhaps it is as well that he died when he was still pouring out song and poem and poetry—what amazing creative vitality he had! I would have hated to see him fade away gradually. He died, as he should, in the fullness of his glory.
>
> I have met many big people in various parts of the world. But I have no doubt in my mind that the two biggest I have had the privilege of meeting have been Gandhi and Tagore. I think they have been the two outstanding personalities in the world during the last quarter of a century. As time goes by, I am sure this will be recognised, when all the generals and field-marshals and dictators and shouting politicians are long dead and largely forgotten.
>
> It amazes me that India in spite of her present condition (or is it because of it?) should produce these two mighty men in course of one generation. And that also convinces me of the deep vitality of India and I am filled with hope, and the petty troubles and conflicts of the day seem very trivial and unimportant before this astonishing fact—the continuity of the idea that is India from long ages past to the present day.

> China affects me in the same way. India and China! How can they perish?
>
> There is another aspect which continually surprises me. Both Gurudev and Gandhiji took much from the West and from other countries, especially Gurudev. Neither was narrowly national. Their message was for the world. And yet both were 100% India's children, and the inheritors, representatives and expositors of her age-long culture. How intensely Indian both have been, in spite of all their wide knowledge and culture! The surprising thing is that both of these men with so much in common and drawing inspiration from the same wells of wisdom and thought and culture, should differ from each other so greatly! No two persons could probably differ so much as Gandhi and Tagore!

Today when we are grappled by the cancer of corruption in the country we remember the three icons of the last century India: Tagore, Gandhi and Nehru who epitomised uprightness and integrity of purpose. It is poignant therefore to end my remarks with a quote from 'Duhsamay', which Tagore recited in Oxford in 1930. The English version reads:

> Though the evening treads in softly,
> And all music is signalled to a stop,
> Though the endless skies are lonely
> And weariness descends on every limb,
> A great fear counts its silent beads
> And all around is a thickening veil,
> Yet O bird, mine bird,
> Do not, sightless, furl your wings!

Sarat Chandra Bose and Rabindranath Tagore

I would like to make a brief, critical assessment of the interaction between Rabindranath Tagore and Sarat Chandra Bose. The element of criticality pertains to Bose's internal dilemma of having to balance Gandhi's view on the non-cooperation movement against that of his brother Subhas Chandra Bose—essentially around the Bengal-India emphasis. Where did Tagore position himself in the complex dynamics of four great individuals—Sarat, Subhas, Gandhi and Rabindranath—all four immensely patriotic in their own ways? There will be two paradigmical issues around which I would like to project this dynamics: one, the travails of Bengali political prisoners in the Andamans, and two, the interpretation of the song 'Vande Mataram' along communal angles.

To do this, let me make a few biographical notes about Sarat Bose. The senior Bose was about 28 years younger than Tagore (and hence about 20 years younger than Gandhi) and 8 years senior to Subhas. After studying in Presidency College, Sarat went to England to become a barrister. That year was indeed significant. Curzan's attempt to divide Bengal had awakened the Bengali mind. The Poet had been emotionally stirred by this draconian act of dismembering Bengal—his pen was the vehicle of his strong sentiments. Sarat returned from England to join the non-cooperation movement of the Indian National Congress. It seems to me that Sarat was torn between the two distinct approaches—one was the peaceful Gandhian movement and the other was the revolutionary zeal of Bengal nationalists. One instance of Sarat's undeclared sympathy for the rebels was his gesture to defend the accused in the robbery of Chittagong armoury free of cost in the British courts of law.

Allow me to fast-forward a bit. The ten years of 1936–1946 may be considered the pinnacle of Sarat Bose's active political life during which he was in close contact with Tagore's idea of nationalism. Between 1937 and 1939 Sarat Bose was the President of Bengal Pradesh Congress Committee, the emphasis of which must be differentiated from that of the Indian National Congress. The latter was grappling with the complex non-uniformity of the Indian subcontinent, the necessity of a single national language, renunciation of foreign products, the need for a new economic policy, the confusion on whether to support the colonial power of Britain, pitted against the trio of Germany, Italy and Japan in what became the Second World War, and so on.

On the other hand, the special problem of Bengal pertained to the Hindu-Muslim divide, the British atrocity on political prisoners in the Andamans, etc. In this regard we find a union between the views of Sarat and Rabindranath. Gurudev was close to the poor Muslim fishermen and weavers that he encountered in Silaidaha. He felt that the 'Charkha' policy of Gandhi was in fact detrimental to the interest of the poor weavers. In a national meeting, held on 20 March of 1937 in Delhi, which Sarat Bose presided over, Tagore sent a strong message, in support of the political prisoners of Bengal. On 2 August of 1937 there was a large assembly of agitated Bengalis in the Town Hall in demand for the release of political prisoners from the Andaman jails. Tagore readily agreed to preside over the meeting at the request of Sarat Bose. Tagore's voice wavered while delivering the presidential speech. He said:

> I am not a politician—my limited role is to appeal for justice and humane approach to the plight of our prisoners languishing in the jails of the Andamans. More than two hundred prisoners have been fasting in the jails.

Here Tagore draws a distinction between the policies of the Indian government and the Bengal provincial government. He asked:

> Why were only Bengali political prisoners subjected to inhuman and discriminating treatment than the other prisoners in the rest of the country?

Tagore, in his speech, made it amply clear that the Bengal issue was quite different from the Indian one—and Sarat Bose was fully in consonance with this concept—and that was not quite in tune with Gandhi's pan-Indian point of view.

One other issue which brings to the fore the unanimity of the thought processes of Tagore and Bose concerns an essay on 'Bande Mataram', written by Krishna Kripalani in a Visva-Bharati publication, on 19 October 1937.

The conservative Hindus of Bengal felt that Kripalani, being critical of 'Bande Mataram', was trying to placate Muslim sentiments. Tagore and Bose however maintained their compassionate neutral stance vis-à-vis the Hindus and the Muslims. On this, *The Amrita Bazar Patrika* wrote on 27 October 1937:

> After granting 'Darshan' to the crowd at Woodburn Park where he is staying as Mr Sarat Bose's guest, Mahatmaji left in a car to meet Poet R.N. Tagore at his suburban residence at Belgharia. The scene of this meeting between the two great souls was very touching indeed and the sight of this aged and infirm Poet running forward with feeble steps to clasp the saint of Shegaon in loving embrace was worthy of the Gods to see.
>
> After preliminary exchange of greetings, Mahatmaji conveyed felicitations of the nation to the Poet on his being spared to them through the last great crisis. Then these two master minds, it is gathered, talked about several burning issues agitating the country at present, particularly the communal situation in Bengal in the light of Moslem agitation against the C.U. emblem and the 'Bande Mataram' song. The Poet it is learnt, opened out his heart to Mahatmaji and made several valuable suggestions for

> the guidance of the national movement in the present deplorable situation which he opined was a mere passing phase and should be endured since it could not be cured immediately.

Tagore told Jawarharlal Nehru that only the first stanza of 'Bande Mataram' would be sung in the Congress meetings, and that way he helped avoid hurting the Muslim sentiments. In this regard, both Tagore and Sarat Bose were the epitome of secularism and the unity of Bengal for which Bose was even willing to join hands with Surhawardy in order to preserve the territorial integrity of Bengal. In a press statement issued on 6 September of 1937, Tagore said:

> The foreign power may derive delight by maligning Bengalis and driving a fissure between its warring communities but when our own people fall prey to this machination, I feel pained. I have struggled all my life to uphold the dignity of Bengal. I therefore feel only dialogues can pave the path of rapprochement between factional tendencies.

In this context the poet was critical of reports published in *The Amrita Bazar Patrika*, which he viewed as divisive. About Sarat Bose, we are told:

> Sarat Bose believed in complete independence of India, independence undiluted and undefiled, free from British or any other foreign influence and control, beyond the reach of any power on earth.

A year before his death, Bose wrote in 1949:

> Socialism alone is the cure for our country's ills; the right-wing Congress leadership's blundering policy has led the country from one form of slavery to another and is sure to bring complete political and economic ruin of the country.

L-R: Rabindranath Tagore, Sarat Chandra Bose and Subhas Chandra Bose in Mahajati Sadan

Summarizing then, both Tagore and Sarat Bose were bonded to the Bengal identity, communal harmony, secularism and socialism that ought to embrace equity and justice. No wonder Tagore composed:

> *Banglar mati Banglar jol. Banglar bayu, Banglar phol*
> *Amar shonar Bangla, ami tomai bhalobashi*
> (O Lord, please bless
> Bengal's soil, Bengal's water, Bengal's air, Bengal's fruit
> My golden Bengal—I adore thee

In conclusion, I would like to narrate what Mrs Chitra Ghosh, the youngest daughter of Sarat Chandra Bose, told me. When Tagore was desperate to raise money for Visva-Bharati to save it from bankruptcy, he appealed to Bose as well. Unfortunately Sarat was in Jail and Tagore passed away within a year of making this plea and therefore, Sarat Bose's effort to help Visva-Bharati never got fructified.

Ashutosh Mukherjee and Tagore, on Education

Today we are talking about the need for taking some of our universities to world class. Our leaders and educationists have often lamented about none of our universities to be of that class. The issue has become perhaps more acute in the background of emerging universities in Asia, specifically in China, Korea and Singapore, which have been aggressively pursuing a system of excelling in all the ranking yardsticks that make universities world class. In this regard, it is clear that the United States of America, which can boast of top universities, actively encourage enrolment of foreign students and employment of best faculty from all over the world. Indeed, the presence of foreign faculty and students in the university system is an important parameter in ranking universities.

In this context, Professor Ashutosh Mukherjee and his visionary approach as Vice Chancellor of Calcutta University, stand out as exemplary and contemporarily relevant. Even though we were under the British Raj, Sir Ashutosh went out of his way and showed great farsightedness in attracting faculty from all over the country. Two notable instances are those of Sir C.V. Raman, who was appointed as Palit Professor of Physics, and Dr Sarvapalli Radhakrishnan, who was invited to a Philosophy Chair. Mind you, Raman was working, not in any educational institute earlier, but as an amateur scientist working part-time on research, away from his duties in the Calcutta Mint. Again, Sir Ashutosh demonstrated courage of conviction and ability to take risks, a rare quality these days amongst our rule-observing Vice Chancellors.

Two contemporaries of Mukherjee, Rabindranath Tagore and Madan Mohan Malaviya, also had the same approach in their bid to build two outstanding universities of India: Visva-Bharati (Santiniketan) and Banaras Hindu University (Varanasi). Tagore went further in inviting great scholars like Leonard Elmhirst (for developing Agricultural Sciences), Tan Yun Shan (for establishing the Cheena-Bhavana), Okakura (for helping promote Japanese studies in Nippon-Bhavana), and so on. A large number of foreign students and students from other parts of the country thronged the Visva-Bharati campus, enriching its academic and cultural atmosphere. Similarly, Malaviya opened the door of BHU to scholars from East, South and West of India, making the campus a cosmopolitan one. Alas, we have reduced our heritage universities to provincial levels, by an exclusive approach that smacks of insecurity.

Coming back to Sir Ashutosh, he actively encouraged research in the university, being a Mathematician of substance himself. Thus, under his patronage, Raman went on to win the Nobel Prize in Physics, the first in science in Asia, on his path-breaking work on Raman Spectroscopy. He integrated the Asiatic Society and the Science Congress Association of Calcutta to promote research among the faculty of Calcutta University. Today, we seem to feel that universities can only do teaching while higher form of research can be relegated to national laboratories. We need to resurrect Sir Ashutosh's concepts to rejuvenate research in our university system.

At present we are concerned about certain Indian languages which are on the verge of extinction. The University Grants Commission has dubbed them as 'Endangered Languages'. Though Sanskrit, Pali, Prakrit do not fall in this category, these aforesaid languages are also 'endangered' because of lack of interest. Once again, we should remember Sir Ashutosh in promoting the study of Indian languages in Calcutta University as a way of linking to our Eastern heritage and not be swayed by colonial prejudices.

Though Sir Ashutosh began his career as a pure mathematician he went on to become an outstanding legal luminary. Thus, he himself was an 'integrated' persona who could therefore stress the importance of interdisciplinary studies in Calcutta University, another crying need for the present approach to education. Hence, we ought to remember Sir Ashutosh Mukherjee, not just as a great institution builder but also as a model educationist.

Rabindranath Tagore with Victoria Ocampo

The Buenos Aires Travelogue

It all started a year ago in Tianjin, China, when the next meeting of The World Academy of Sciences (TWAS) was announced to be scheduled in Buenos Aires. I had already joined as Vice-Chancellor of Visva-Bharati, about a year ago. Naturally, the Tagore-connection with Buenos-Aires (and Argentina, in general) triggered a special interest in my mind; I felt, it would be interesting to travel to Buenos Aires, a very long and arduous journey notwithstanding.

The acronym TWAS has an added suffix that reads: 'for the developing world'. TWAS, was established by the great Pakistani/Indian physicist Abdus Salam. (The subcontinent was not partitioned when Salam was born.) Though Salam went on to win the Nobel Prize in Physics for his monumental contribution in elucidating the fundamental forces of nature, his biggest legacy to my mind is the translation of his deep concern for science in the developing world (of Africa, Asia and Latin America) into the creation of International Centre for Theoretical Physics (ICTP). Located in the northern Italian city of Trieste, ICTP is situated in the seductive surroundings of the Adriatico Sea, flanked by the beautiful Miramare Castle. Over the years ICTP has helped generations of third world scientists, in terms of state-of-the-art library and computational facilities as well as visitors' programmes. I myself have tremendously benefitted in my research work through several visits to ICTP as Associate and Senior Associate, in the eighties and nineties.

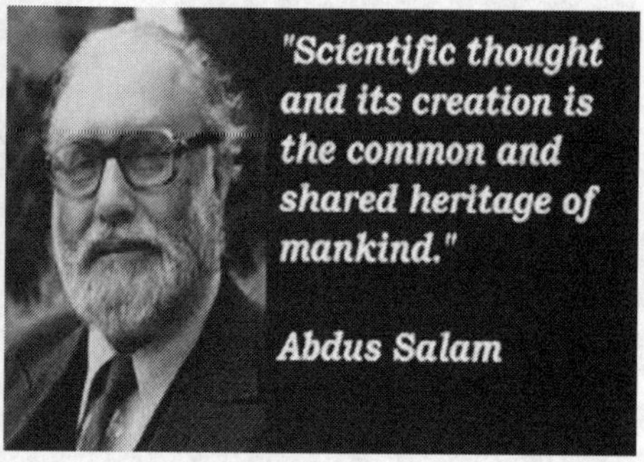

Left: *International Centre of Theoretical Physics (ICTP), in Trieste*
Right: *Pakistan–Indian physicist Abdus Salam*

Quite appropriately then, TWAS was called 'The Third World Academy of Sciences', when Salam had founded it, also in Trieste. Unlike other academies of sciences that are country-specific, TWAS is unique—it caters to the countries of the south as well as the north. I was fortunate to be elected to TWAS membership in 1999, which had given me an opportunity to interact with myriad scientists from all parts of the world, with diverse nationalities and cultures. Additionally, the icing on the cake has been the sojourn to some wonderful corners of the world, starting with Tehran, Shiraj and Ishpahan (along with an unforgettable trip to the ruins of Parsepolis), and then Beijing, Angra dos Reis (Brazil), Durban (South Africa), Mexico City, Tianjin and now Buenos Aires.

Remarkably and coincidentally, when my secretary Ms Shyamala Ray Nair was filling-in various TWAS forms on my behalf, came an e-mail from the Indian Ambassador to Argentina—Shri Amarendra Khatua. The Ambassador wanted me to help a certain professor from Buenos Aires, Gustavo Canzobre, visit Santiniketan. Gustavo came early this year, and almost in the wake of that visit occurred a seminar on Tagore and Ocampo, organised by Professor Tapati Mukhopadhyay and Professor Amrit Sen of Rabindra-Bhavana. The key speaker at that seminar was my former Jawaharlal Nehru University colleague from the Department of Spanish—Professor S.P. Ganguly—another lucky coincidence. SP or Shamu, as we call him, enthralled us with a vivid description of the Tagore–Ocampo meet in Buenos Aires in 1924! Shamu also donated to Rabindra-Bhavana several

memorabilia of that extraordinary personality, named Victoria Ocampo. It seems the only good thing that Visva-Bharati had done in the past was to honour Ocampo with its highest award: Desikottama. I say this because Shamu lamented that several attempts by Ocampo's secretary to hand over her personal effects to Visva-Bharati had fallen on deaf ears of the then authorities. Sad indeed, as it seems that Visva-Bharati had been insensitive, not for the first time though, to record one of history's most significant encounters, between Ocampo and Tagore. More about that later.

As Shamu rekindled my interest in visiting Buenos Aires, Shyamala contacted Gustavo. Gustavo now runs the Hastinapur Foundation in Buenos Aires. As the name and its connotation to the *Mahabharata* would suggest, the Hastinapur Foundation deals with East-West confluence of philosophical and spiritual issues. As Gustavo later mentioned, the West appears to be unidirectional and exclusive, as far as soul-searching is concerned. It is the East that offers a more balanced point of view in terms of an inclusive approach to accommodating diverse ideas.

After initial hiccups about getting the Argentinian visa, a process that was also helped by Gustavo's kind intervention, I was off to Buenos Aires

The TWAS meeting, held in a big and posh (but very impersonal, as far as services were concerned) hotel, was enjoyable as I was back to my familiar groove of hard sciences. One symposium, devoted to quantum information was personally informative, as the topic is close to my present research interest, thanks to an on-going collaboration with my Israeli friends. The TWAS meeting was also nice in that I could meet with many familiar faces from all over the globe. One aspect is worth mentioning; I have always found it rewarding to talk to scientists from Pakistan, whom we cannot normally see, because of artificially erected barriers. The Pakistanis are warm and polite, and are so similar to us in our liking of music, food, etc., that I find it strange that we have been rudely separated by the whims of history!

After four days of science, with occasional forays to the city, distinguished by its massively broad avenues, I was finally ready for Gustavo, on 5 October morning. Three of my Bengali scientist friends accompanied, and off we

A visit to 'Villa Ocampo'

were in Gustavo's French car to the 'Villa Ocampo'. The story that Gustavo narrated on the way through some really scenic roads, adorned by tall (and old) trees on both sides was absorbing and fascinating, to say the least.

Apparently, Gurudev Tagore (on that famous sea-voyage to Latin America in 1924) did not know Victoria Ocampo at all. He was accompanied by Leonard Elmhirst, one of the pioneers of the rural reconstruction project of Sriniketan, and when they reached the port city of Rio de Jeneiro of Brazil, Tagore was struck by influenza. They were earlier planning to ride a train through the Andeas in a cross-country trip to Lima, Peru, for attending a commemorative convocation. However, the flu-stricken Tagore was so sick that he was advised to be taken to Buenos Aires. (Gustavo said in jest that the whole of Argentina is grateful to that flu virus which had attacked Tagore!). He was booked in the Plaza hotel, not far from the Sheraton where we had the TWAS meeting. Ocampo lived about 50 km away, but rushed in to see Gurudev. She had read the French translation of *Gitanjali*, shortly after her own marriage to a famous Argentinian Lawyer in

Rabindranath Tagore with Ocampo at the Galarie Pigalle, Paris

1912 broke off, interestingly on the honeymoon night. Ocampo, born in 1890, was so moved by reading *Gitanjali* that it was impossible for her to not to look up Tagore.

Victoria Ocampo was an unusual woman. She was exquisitely attractive with chiselled features. Though a product of a rich, conservative family, she was a liberated and emancipated young person who had defied society by wearing pants and smoking in public. When she saw Gurudev in his pitiable physical condition, she immediately offered to take him to her villa, 50 km away in a more congenial and quiet surrounding.

There was one hitch though—her father put his foot down—he won't let a male, foreigner live in the same house! What did Victoria do? She went to an elderly relation who had owned a house, four blocks away, towards the river, and rented it from him for a week. Tagore and Elmhirst moved-in, aided by a retinue of Ocampo's chefs and servants.

According to Gustavo, Tagore's initial reaction to his arrival in Argentina was intriguing. He had expected to meet 'Gauchos' on the streets

Rabindranath Tagore with Ocampo at his feet

of Buenos Aires; instead he was welcomed by a modern European-type city, built by French and Italian architects. He, however, loved the salubrious environment, further enriched by Victoria's captivating hospitality and charm. Rabindranath was 63 years old then—Victoria was 34. By that time she was an accomplished writer, mostly in French, though she knew English and Spanish well, apparently in that order. She was also a gifted pianist; the large piano in the middle of her study in Villa Ocampo is a living testimony to her musical skills. What was to be a week's stay for Tagore became two months; this was much to the glee of Rabindranath, who did not seem to mind the prolongation of the virus-affliction. But how did Victoria afford the extended stay? It is said that she sold off her pearl necklace!

We were greeted at the Ocampo villa by a young Argentinian girl who had a broad smile—she spoke fluent English. She guided us through the Villa on a sunny day, through the lovely gardens, surrounded by tall and elegant trees. Because the season was early spring, the air was crisp and cold, adding to the aura of the place. We were led to the main house and were immediately awe-struck by the tastefully arranged furniture.

Victoria liked white-painted doors and windows but she had left some of the doors in their original teak facade. By the time her father died and the conservative shackles were removed, she had many of her close friends—the writers Camus and Virginia Wolf and the music-maestro Stravinsky—all come and stay with her. The Villa Ocampo was also visited by the famous Indian philosopher J. Krishnamurthy, who himself was influenced by the Santiniketan model of education when he had created his schools in Chittoor and Varanasi.

The living room in which many of these luminaries would gather around to discuss their creative experiences is adorned with famous photographs, most prominent of them being Tagore's. That Tagore had a very special place in Ocampo's life is apparent by the insignia of the Villa Ocampo—a book-marker that has Rabindranath seated in a garden chair with her disciple Victoria sitting at his feet. What did they discuss? Everything: the Eastern philosophies of Upanishada and Gita, the Puranic stories, Western civilisation, Latin American identity, the liberation of

Potrait of Ocampo by Rabindranath Tagore

Argentina from the Spaniards, and so on. These were no-holds-barred, frank and long intellectual discourses that brought these two greatly gifted individuals together. The young guide marvelled at describing this extraordinary relationship as though she was living through it.

What on earth can explain this union of two absolute strangers, coming from two nations with very different cultures and moorings, the younger one knowing the older one only through his writings? Can there be any other form of love that is deeper than this spiritual intersection of these two remarkable human beings?'

Tagore named Victoria 'Vijaya'; mind you, spelt with a V in front and not a B, the usual Bengali way of initialising the name 'Bijoya'. I take it that Tagore literally transcribed Victoria, which connotes victory, into Vijaya, the Sanskrit word that relates to Vijay—victory. Perhaps he was mindful of the Indo-European language-link that connected Sanskrit to Latin! He dedicated his book of poems *Purabi* to his loving Vijaya.

Vijaya lent brushes and paints to the convalescing Tagore, who, in moments of inspiration, began his sojourn into another facet of his creative endeavour—painting. The Tagore paintings—about 2000 in number—carry with them the imprints of another side of his genius. One can experience that through *Chitrabali*, a Pratikshan/Visva-Bharati publication, helped by my Kala-Bhavana colleague, Professor Raman Sivakumar. Six years later, after that historical rendezvous in Buenos Aires, Gurudev and Victoria met again in Paris. Gurudev was a rejuvenated self, inspired by his dialogues with Albert Einstein, and embarking on writing his book on science, called *Visva Parichay*, but was also interested in introducing his paintings to European connoisseurs. Ocampo came with help: with her very strong contacts with the French intelligentsia, Victoria assisted Tagore in putting up an exhibition in Paris. By that time, Tagore was of course a famous name because of his writings, the Nobel Prize and his wise statesmanship. The instant success of the exhibition helped promote another one in Berlin.

I know of no other episode in the history of this world which has witnessed such an extraordinary communion of two outstanding genii who broke all hindrances of age, culture, language and upbringing, to have come so close to each other, to enrich themselves and us, for posterity.

The Indian connection also came in handy for Ocampo. When the senior Juan Perón, dictatorial those days, had imprisoned Victoria Ocampo in the fifties, being intolerant of her liberal and outspoken political views (like those of Tagore), what helped liberate her was none other than a strongly worded letter from the then Indian Prime Minister, Pandit Jawaharlal Nehru. Perón was keen to make Argentina a part of Nehru's non-aligned movement and he could simply not ignore Jawaharlal's impassioned plea. I take pride, as a part of the Visva-Bharati fraternity, in this unusually thoughtful gesture of my first Chancellor, just as I rejoice in the fact that another of my ex-'Acharya'—Prime Minister Indira Gandhi—personally went to Villa Ocampo to present Victoria with the Desikottama award. Jawaharlal and Indira also contribute to the photo gallery of the Villa. Victoria never could visit Santiniketan, but emulated the Visva-Bharati

Quarterly by creating the Sur magazine. She lived up to 89 years until 1979; but before her passing, she was so petrified by the thought of her property being impounded by the Argentinian authorities that she donated her Villa Ocampo to UNESCO. It now runs as a museum—a tribute to this unusual, non-conformist and intellectual genius who did so much for international understanding and for bringing together two disparate nations, Argentina and India, because of her dedicated admiration for the greatest Indian, in my opinion, who had set foot on this earth.

I came back to Buenos Aires on the evening of 5 October, thanking my stars, TWAS, Gustavo Canzobre and last but not least, Ambassador Khatua and his able assistant, the second Secretary Suhashini Narayanan, for making possible this memorable visit that I shall cherish for the rest of my life. What can we do from Visva-Bharati to keep reminding us of this rich Tagore-Ocampo legacy? For one, as we discussed over the sumptuous Mexican dinner that Khatua hosted for me on the 4th evening, we must strive to enhance the Latin American understanding of Tagore through more vigorous translation of his works in Spanish, bringing in Rabindrasangeet and Sangeet-Bhavana to the Argentinian people through the cultural centre that the Ambassador is planning to create, and through that, propagate the message of universal love and human bondage that Rabindranath Tagore had personified.

Purabi—A Background

Rabindranath had his book of poems *Purabi* published in the year 1925, a year after his famous meeting with Victoria Ocampo. Most of the poems of *Purabi* were written between 26 September 1924 and 24 January 1925—recall that the Bard arrived in Rio on 19 September and landed in Buenos Aires on 6 November. So we can easily conclude that *Purabi* was inspired by Argentina, and specially, Victoria, whom Tagore called Vijaya. Tagore wrote in the dedication: *To Vijoya's lotus-hands*. It is pertinent to mention that *Purabi* is in two parts—'Purabi' and 'Pathik'—The Traveller. Though the Argentina-based writings are contained in 'Pathik', the Ocampo encounter is subsumed by *Purabi*.

It is important to dwell on the meaning of 'Purabi'. 'Purabi' is an evening raga of Hindustani classical music, signalling the onset of the dusk. How did the Poet view this raga? Well, to him, Purabi is akin to the shedding of tears by a lonely, homebound widow, called 'Evening'.

Why did Tagore associate melancholy with evening? He wrote in 'Atma-Katha: Chinnapatrabali' on 15 December 1895:

> We would often go on boat rides on the Padma at the sunset. Jyotidada would play the violin to my tunes. As we would transit from *Purabi to Behaag* the golden disc on the western sky would have made way for the arrival of the silvery moon on the

eastern horizon. Yesterday when we were gradually returning in our jolly-boat in the midst of the golden dusk my heart was suddenly filled with violin-rendition of the *Alaap* of *Purabi*, emanating from a distant, invisible boat. My heart was entirely submerged within the intersection of the motionless river and the still sky. I felt, there is nothing comparable to the tune of *Purabi* that epitomises the astonishing and infinitely exquisite beauty of the dusk—this indeed was another facet of the marvel of creation. The enchanting raga of *Purabi* easily got enmeshed with the enigmatic charm of the evening-time—my inner self was completely satiated with this extraordinary unification of nature and melody.

The above mentioned feeling is encapsulated in 'Lilasangini' of *Purabi*:

Dekha na ki, hai, bela chole jai,
Shara hoye elo din
Baje Purobir chhonde Robir
Shesh raginir been

In a letter to Ocampo from Calcutta, on 29 October 1925, almost a year after his trip to Buenos Aires, Tagore scribbled:

Dear Vijaya,

I am sending to you a Bengali book of poems which I wish I could place in your hand personally. I have dedicated it to you though you will never be able to know what it contains. A large number of poems in this book were written while I was in San Isidro. My readers who will understand these poems will never know who my Vijaya is with whom they are associated. I hope this book will have the chance of larger time with you than its author had. Bhalobasha,
Sri Rabindranath Thakur.

What did Ocampo think of *Purabi*? In her own words:

> When Tagore lived in San Isidro I was impressed by the copy-book where he was writing his *Purabi* poems in Bengali. He played with the erasures, following them from verse to verse with his pen, making lines that suddenly jumped into life out of this play: prehistoric monsters, birds, faces appeared. The cancelled mistakes in Tagore's poems gave birth to a world of forms that grinned, frowned or laughed at us in a mysterious and fascinating way. I begged him to let me photograph some of the pages. The permission was granted. That copy-book, I think, was the beginning of Tagore the Painter, of his urge to translate his dreams with a pencil or a brush. I took such delight in his doodles that it encouraged him to go on. When I met him, six years later, in France, he was painting, not doodling, and the exhibition I arranged for him with the help of my French friends was a success.

She further added:

> The debt that I, a westerner and South American, owe to men like Gandhiji and Gurudev is like the restitution of a treasure I had inherited without being aware of it. They have opened for me, as for many others, the doors of perception which, if they remain hermetically closed, separate us from reality. By reality I mean the following: the triviality of the finite, like the emptiness of the infinite, are no more than false appearances. These false appearances (Dante's 'falso imaginare') may distort our view of all things and transform the world into hell. Blessed be those who help us if not to escape completely from this hell, at least to unlock the doors through which escape is possible. During his stay at San Isidro, Tagore taught me a few words of Bengali. I have retained only one, which I shall always repeat to India: *Bhalobasa*.

From this song and the background to its composition we can surmise that 'Videshini' is not any specific foreign lady, just as in one other song: *'Shunil shagore shyamolo kinare...'* In this song 'Tulonahina' or the Incomparable is an artistic imagination of the Poet—the Videshini and the Tulonahina are one and the same. The Bard had experienced the familiar figure of a stranger woman through his music—just as an artist paints and gives shape to his objects of deep feelings.

It is however interesting to note that Ocampo herself found her mirror image in the form of a Videshini. She wrote:

> I knew who Tagore was and his books had told me about him things that his actual presence now made complete. But Tagore could know nothing of the speechless creature I was except by intuition. 'I know you, O woman from a strange land! Your dwelling is across the sea...' Did my silence really tell him my thoughts? I am afraid it did not and that our knowledge of each other was extremely one-sided. If I regret it, it is only because he could never have known how close to him that 'woman from a strange land' was, how these two lands were, against all appearances, close to each other in spite of the oceans and climates. He could never have known that listening to those songs which came 'across the sea', I seemed to anticipate the words of our great western poet, St. John Perse: 'Here I am restored to my native shore. There is no history but of the soul.

Quite like the 'Videshi Phul' the 'Foreign Flower' there is a similar poem 'Atithi' from *Purabi*.

> WOMAN, thou hast made my days of exile tender with beauty,
> And hast accepted me to thy nearness with a simple grace
> That is like the smile with which the unknown star welcomed me
> When I stood alone at the balcony and gazed upon the southern night.

> There came the voice from above: "We know you,
> For you come as our guest from the dark of the infinite, the guest of light."
> Even in the same great voice thou hast cried to me: "I know you."
> And though I know not thy tongue, Woman, I have heard it uttered in thy music,—
> "You are ever our guest on this earth, poet, and the guest of love."

Why the Poet viewed Raga Purabi as one of sadness is worth noting. The dusk, which is associated with Purabi, comes in the wake of the day—and it is the day that is blessed with the sun, the source of all energy and life-forms of this world. The sun has played a central role in Tagore's psyche—in his entire Upanishadic assessment of the interaction, through nature, between Man and the Creator. The embodiment of the sun in the Poet's soul is inseparably embedded in the coincidental naming of himself as a child—'Robi'. The Bard has been eloquent in eulogising the sun in his poem 'Sabitri' from *Purabi*.

In *Paschim Yatrir Diary* (The Diary of the West-bound Voyager) Tagore penned his appreciation of nature, on 26 September 1924:

> Today the Sun is sporadically peeping through the cloud cover as though He is bashfully hesitant to come out of the window-grills—He seems to be under the watchful surveillance of the black-uniformed cloud-sentries of the Rain-God! My own stream of senses is subdued as it is ebbed by the dim sunlight—I am made to await the occurrence of the tidal wave in my body due to the full-blown sunlight…I have seen in the West man does not feel the intimate presence of the Sun in his veins for obvious reasons of climate conditions. But for us, in the East, our entire existences—our pleasures…are sourced in that great star. Wasn't the entire evolutionary process of the solar system embedded in that original fire ball? Wasn't the same sunlight propagating through the cells of my body, my consciousness…

like waves? It is the spectrum of that white light that lends colour to all external objects and our 'agony and ecstasy'. It is that bright illumination which conveys such beauty, such feeling, such emotion. It is that light energy which seems to be collected as nectar in a bunch of grapes. Indeed, it is that energy which gets manifested as melody in my numerous songs. Isn't it the same sunlight which is absorbed in the leaves and branches of trees that is also responsible for the translation into language of all my inner ideas?

Oh, my Sun-Lord—our mother earth is incessantly paying obeisance to your glory through its leaves, grasses and trees—it is constantly pleading to you to uncover the lid just as a flower uncovers itself to develop into a fruit. It is this art of uncovering of light that is at the very genesis of the evolution of man—from worms to higher forms of life, and now, it is the same lightwave that helps me to transit from my body to my mind, my cognitive senses. I raise my hands to you in prayer to plead with you—please remove the lid of your golden pot, allow my inner truth to experience your limitless and unbounded energy—let me vibrate in resonance with you.

The poem 'Anmona go, anmona' from *Purabi*, was written on 18 October 1924, a month after 'Sabitri' (26 September 1924) and 'Akashbhora' (17 September 1924):

My heart feels shy to bring to your
Vagrant mind
The lyric of my secret lest its meaning
Be missed
And its rhythm.
I shall wait for some auspicious hour
When the evening is compassionate,
Your eyes drowned in its tender dimness,

And my voice reaches you
In a profound calm of truth.
I shall turn my secret round and round
Through my whisper
At a lonely corner of your heart,
Even as the cricket among the silent
Sal trees
Turns single-toned beads of its chirping
In the rosary of night

'Bodol' ('The Exchange'), also from *Purabi,* written on 17 January 1925, and its English translation by Kshitis Roy, on 8 May 1960:

She brought me flowers of joy
And I had with me
The fruits of my sorrow.
Who will be the loser
I asked her,
If we exchange?

Amused and smiling
She said,
Come on then, let us.
My garland is yours,
I shall accept
Your fruit of pain.

I looked up at her face
And saw that she was pitiless
In her beauty.

She clapped her hands
In glee,

And picked up
My basket of fruits,
While I held to my heart
Her garland of flowers.
I win,
Smiling said she
As in a moment
She flitted away.
The Sun rose
To the mid-heaven
And it was burning hot.
At the sultry end
Of the day
All the flowers withered
And shed their petals.

The abstract imagination of Tagore of a distant damsel from overseas keeps haunting him in his poetry and music. The song '*Ogo amar chiro-ochena porodeshi*' which we sing in 'Borshamongol' was composed by the Poet when he was seventy-six years old and has glimpses of the indelible impression that Victoria Ocampo left in Tagore's mind, according to his biographer Probhatkumar Mukhopadhyay.

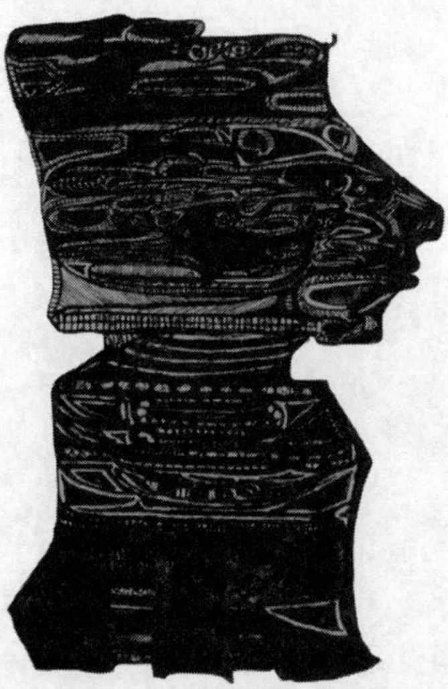

A page from the manuscript of Purabi

The poem 'Panchishe Boisakh' written in 1922, two years before the Poet's Argentina jaunt, is however contained in *Purabi*. We include this poem (and its English translation by Indira Devi Choudhurani), first published on 8 May 1945, as it symbolises certain recurring themes that keep coming back in the mind of the roaming Poet, who was ever so dynamic. Indeed, the song rendition of 'Panchishe Boisakh' was carried out by the Bard at the request of Acharya Shanti Dev Ghosh, on the Poet's final birthday, celebrated in Santiniketan. The song version has a few alterations from the original form, published in 1922.

O Ever-New,
Let the auspicious moment of thy birth
Appear again. Buried it lies beneath
The dusty worn-out leaves of shrunken seconds.
O new-comer,
Remember that the first day of thy birth
Is changeless; like unto the waterfall
That's reborn every minute; like the sea
That is revived in waves unceasingly,
O newly-born, may thy awakening be
Like fire that springs from ashes dazzlingly.
O Ever-New,
Let thy appearance, like the morning Sun,
Roll back all mists. Or like the tender shoots
—The standard-bearers of victorious spring—
That fill the empty branches of the forest
In one swift moment, mayest thou, new one,
Breaking through arid wastes, thyself reveal,
Through thee may life's all-conquering be exprest,
Through thee revealed
The quenchless wonder of the Infinite.
The whiter conch blows upon the sunrise line,
Vaisakh,the twenty-fifth
Calls to the ever-new within my heart.

The Tokyo Travelogue

I do not know of any other occasion in which the Upacharya of Visva-Bharati had been on a 'State' visit at the invitation of the Ministry of Foreign Affairs (MOFA) of Japan! The Japan trip, planned for 8 October 2013, was going to be characteristically distinct from anything I had undertaken in my professional career in India. The serious elaborateness of the preparation for the visit had not dawned on me earlier; it was my affable secretary, Ms Shyamala Nair Ray, who had to bear the brunt of the incessant barrage of queries from the Japan Consul's office of Kolkata over the ever-changing schedules that were emanating from discussions between MOFA and the Kolkata consular office.

Incidentally, this was not my first sojourn to Japan. Way back in the spring of 1976, when we were permanently returning to India for starting a career, following doctoral and post-doctoral training in USA and Canada, I had been to Tokyo and Kyoto on a private vacation with my family. I was back in Japan many years later to attend a meeting of the Japan Science Council, in my capacity of the Vice President of International Affairs, of the Indian National Science Academy.

But, as I said before, this trip was going to be quite different—one that I owe to my good fortune of leading a university that was founded by one of Asia's greatest thinkers: Gurudev Rabindranath Tagore. It is also appropriate to acknowledge the unflinching efforts of a most amiable diplomat in the form of Mitsuo Kawaguchi-San, the Consul General of Japan in Kolkata, who was the chief protagonist behind making the arrangements.

Mr Kawaguchi invited us to a lovely dinner on the evening of 26 September, in Salt Lake, just on our way to the Kolkata airport. And, as you might guess, there was Tagore's presence right from the word 'go'. The musician at the restaurant played Rabindrasangeet tunes on violin, one after another, to which Kawaguchi-San hummed in his delightful Japanese accent. I too joined in this Bongo-Japanese harmony, the seeds of which had been sown almost a century ago, when Tagore set foot on Japan, for the first time, in 1916.

Our Thai Airlines flight to Tokyo via Bangkok was a further reminder of what we were trying to recreate in the Lalbandh area—an orchid garden—thanks to the tireless efforts of Shubhashish Mitra, Samiran Nandy, and others. The orchid is the symbol of Thai Airlines that also captures the lively presence of a large number of Thai students who throng Sangeet and Kala-Bhavanas of Visva-Bharati. Thus, as we were approaching the Narita airport, we were adequately soaked in a Santiniketan mindset, waiting expectantly for what we had been told before—Japan's renewed interest in India, in the background of historically strong ties that dated back to the propagation of Buddhism, to the establishment of silk route, and so on.

We were met at the airport by an efficient-looking Japanese guide, Ms Michio Yoko, and an impeccably attired chauffeur, Mr Hara, who came in a black Toyota limousine, carrying an insignia of the Japanese government. They were going to be our inseparable companions during the week-long stay. What unfolded soon was a glimpse of a society that works on principles diametrically opposite to what we Indians are used to.

I am reminded of what Tagore once said about his own music in contradistinction to Western or even classical Hindustani music. He told the great physicist Albert Einstein in 1930, which has been quoted before:

> There is in human affairs an element of elasticity also—some freedom within a small range, which is for the expression of our personality. It is like the musical system in India which is not so rigidly fixed as is the western music. Our composers give a certain

> definite outline, a system of melody and rhythmic arrangement, and within a certain limit the player can improvise upon it.

Our itinerary was totally ordained by MOFA—and our guide, otherwise friendly, would not deviate an iota from it. Even an apparently innocuous 'adjustment' of viewing a shrine, in between two (scheduled) meetings, was politely evaded. We were now confronted by a highly regimented, disciplined and a clockwork-oiled system that did not know of improvisation—a term that is the hallmark of Indian existence.

Apart from a very animated time at the Tokyo University of Foreign Studies, during which I had the opportunity of addressing in Bengali a bunch of Japanese students under the guidance of two Bengali-speaking Japanese professors, the other visits to two agencies of Japan, RICOH and JICA, were nothing to write home about. At least there was no discernible interest in Tagore and his inspired creation, the Visva-Bharati.

If the day was drab, the evening was enlivened by a most enjoyable dinner at a fancy Japanese restaurant hosted by Mr Maktia Shimokawa, Director General, South-East and South-West Asian Affairs of MOFA. Apart from mouth-watering nabe, sushi and sashimi dishes, the high point of the dinner was the presence of a young Japanese colleague of Makita Shimokawa: Ken Komine. Ken not only spoke in fluent Bengali, imbibed as a Masters student of Economics at Visva-Bharati, but also divulged that his Bengali wife Jayita was also from Santiniketan! We immediately extended a dinner invitation to Ken and Jayita, to which Ken hesitatingly admitted that during their stay in Santiniketan he and Jayita could never go near a Vice-Chancellor, let alone dine with him!

My adrenalin level was soon pumped up by visits to RIKEN Tsukuba and Tokyo universities. These meetings were prompted by my own list of physicists that I had wanted to see, the first and foremost being my former PhD student from the S.N. Bose Centre, Suvankar Chakraborty, who was now a staff scientist at the industrial research lab RIKEN. Suvankar's boss, Professor Yoshinori Tokura, is a famous name in the Materials Science community. He very nicely explained all the on-going activities in the area of 'Emergent Matter Science' that I am most familiar with—I was at my ground-level comfort-zone of hard core condensed matter physics. We had an educative tour through a plethora of machines, each of which was considered to be important to procure at my previous organisation of the Indian Institute of Science Education and Research (IISER) in Kalyani. Thus, if we had struggled to install a single MPMS (Magnetic Property Measurement System) or a PPMS (Physical Property Measurement System), manufactured by Quantum Design, the senior scientist Mosashi Kawasaki showed us an array of them! No wonder the Japanese today are at the top of materials science and its spin-off technologies—in nano systems, super conductivity, quantum Hall devices, and so on.

The afternoon visit to Tokyo University was equally exciting. We were met with by the senior professor, Atsushi Fujimori, who I knew from my S.N. Bose days. Like Tokura and Kawasaki, Fujimori also had come into my space through my young brotherly colleague from Bangalore—Dipankar Das Sarma, or DD, as we affectionately call him. Suvankar himself had been a post doc with DD, and hence this phase of the Tokyo meetings could be referred to as the DD-inspired one! There was an element of ego-boosting, as well, when the head of the physics department in Tokyo University pointed to a book of mine, *A Paradigm Called Magnetism*, adorning their library shelf! Overall, I had the impression that the Japanese were very keen to attract science students from India, including undergraduate ones. Alas, Visva-Bharati was not in their radar, though IISERs and IITs definitely were!

The next morning began with a visit to the Japan Foundation, which deals with teachers of Japanese language from 50 odd countries including India. I, of course, immediately pounced on the possible option of sending our own colleagues from Nippon Bhavan, for further training here, just as I did in my discussion with JICA executives in exhorting them to keep sending more JICA volunteers to Visva-Bharati. I intend to take up these possibilities with my colleague, Ms Gita Keeni, as well as the Japan consul, Kawaguchi-San, upon my return to Santiniketan.

The pre-lunch meeting at the doctoral programme of Nano-Science and Nano-Technology at the University of Tsukuba was most intriguing, to say the least. I met the other Y. Tokura—Yasuhiro, who happened to be a co-author of mine in a recent Physical Review paper with my Israeli colleagues on Quantum Information, though we never had an opportunity to meet face-to-face! The chat with Yasuhiro—a pleasantly warm person—on related topics of physics was most rewarding.

Our next stop was NIMS—the National Institute for Materials Science—where we met with an unusual Bengali physicist, Anirban Bandyopadhyay. Anirban was from Malda and the North-Bengal University and was trained in the PhD programme in Materials Science at the Indian Association for the Cultivation of Science in Jadavpur. He seemed to have flourished in NIMS with a range of experimental projects, including an unusual one of studying the effect of music on protein molecules of human brains. I immediately thought of involving Anirban and his group in our new initiative of Rabindrasangeet Gabeshana Kendra in which we do want to explore overlapping areas of music and physics. Finally the day ended with a visit to the High Energy Accelerator Research Organisation (KEK) at the Tsukuba Science City. The scientists at KEK, who have an active participation at CERN, Geneva, are naturally familiar with a large number of Indian Particle physicists, working at TIFR, SINP, VECC and universities, including my good friends Bikash Sinha and Rohini Godbole. A trip through their detector facility was fascinating indeed.

The Friday morning visit was to the Indian Embassy, where our host was the First Secretary, Mr Abbagani Ramu, who also looks after the India Cultural Centre as its Director. Ramu was kind in his hospitality and treated us to an Indian lunch, thinking perhaps that we would be, by this time, quite tired of Japanese food! We did not quite tell him how we have been relishing Japanese dishes, though we showed equal appreciation for Ramu's thoughtful gesture—I did mention to Ramu how keen we were to further enhance our department of Japanese studies including perhaps the creation of a professorial chair, to which he announced his whole-hearted support, especially because of a reciprocal arrangement of two such chairs in Japan, supported by the Government of India.

Rabindranath Tagore in Japan

Now came the pinnacle of our Japan trip—a visit to the Shibusawa Eiichi museum and the Shibusawa Eiichi Memorial Foundation. This was a real eye-opener. Who was Shibusawa Eiichi? I can paint a fairly accurate picture of him by comparing him to our own Jamshedji Tata. Eiichi lived between 1840 and 1931, his passing marking the onset of the great Manchurian war and the Second World War. Shibusawa was responsible for taking Japan from a feudal society to one of commerce and enterprise. Thus he was the pioneering Japanese entrepreneur, having been the founder of as many as 500 different companies, including hotels, hospitals, educational institutions, and so on. With Jamshedji Tata he began collaboration on cotton industries and set up a sea link between Kobe and Bombay, much to the chagrin of the British East India Company!

Shibusawa Eiichi was an unusual businessman who had championed the virtue of honesty and transparency in commerce, intertwined with empathy for the common man. I began to discover the value system of the East, which I had somewhat superficially concluded earlier to be lacking in the Japanese system. I could not help remembering Acharya Prafulla Chandra Ray, who had lamented the Bengali apathy towards business. Here was an individual who almost single-handedly, and without any formal education, helped take Japan to the height of industrialised success.

It was not surprising then, that one of the most prominent Japanese persons that Tagore called on, during his visit to Japan in 1916, was none other than Shibusawa Eiichi. Tagore came again in 1924 and in 1929, when he had developed a strong kinship with Okakura. He also extracted a donation from Eiichi for his beloved Visva-Bharati. We were privileged to walk on the lawns of the Eiichi home, which had the footprints of Gurudev and Shibusawa and were also witness to the exchange of letters between them. Just as the senior Tata was inspired by Swami Vivekananda to start the Indian Institute of Science in Bangalore, Shibusawa Eiichi was the inspirational figure behind many philanthropies of Japan.

When we came back from our walk in the Eiichi garden, we were met with a most charming personality in the great grandson, the 88 year old Mr Masahide Shibusawa, who is currently the President of the Shibusawa Foundation. He regaled us by narrating his India connections—with Rajmohan Gandhi, Rashbehari Bose, Radha Binod Pal, Netaji Subhas Bose and the latter's lieutenants, Col. Bhonsle and Col. Hassan and umpteen other Indian political figures. It was surprising to hear him speak impeccable English, which, as it turned out, had been acquired during teaching stints in London, Anchorrage and Portland—a usual phenomenon in then-Japanese society. The meeting with the junior Shibusawa was the missing link that I had been craving—a true Japanese with an Eastern identity who had successfully managed to blend Western liberal thoughts—a kind of human being that Tagore would have loved to meet.

Our last day in Japan was spent on sightseeing through the delightful Zen Buddhist and Shinto town of Kamakura. Apart from the mammoth

At a tea ceremony in Japan

Buddha statue, it was fascinating to see the influence of Hindu Gods and Goddesses in their idol forms, just as it was revealing to witness the preponderance of nature—long ginkgo and cherry trees—surrounding the shrines, lending an atmosphere of serenity, perfect for meditation, that is so sadly absent from our noisy temple sites in India.

What is the take-home message from Japan? It is a country that has beaten the Western world hollow in terms of transferring scientific research into technological innovation and becoming an economic superpower, yet maintaining an Eastern identity of family values and traditional philosophy. It is very different from our society and it takes a long time to understand and unravel the true complexity that it is endowed with. If I were awed by the daunting Japanese discipline, I was rudely shaken by the unruly, fellow young Indian travellers, who made their messy presence felt at the Bangkok lounge of Thai Air, and demonstrated their 'at-home' liberation by violating the non-smoking zone of the airport toilet in Kolkata. I said to myself—I probably don't know which lifestyle I prefer. I did know however that I was keen to return to my cocoon, the abode of 'Shanti', in my beloved Santiniketan.

I am grateful to the MOFA and the Japanese consular office, Kolkata, for giving me a glimpse of this fabulous country—a week being too short a time to experience all its intricate ramifications.

Tagore on Science

Tagore, on Science—through Songs

To search for imprints of science in Rabindrasangeet and analyse certain songs of the Bard in the light of modern scientific thoughts, we wanted to see if we could use Tagore's music in science education—in school curriculums as well as in research. This is what we endeavoured to carry out in our newly-developed Rabindrasangeet Gabeshana Kendra.

Tagore explores every marvel of creation through his songs. In *Tumi Kemon Kore Gaan Koro Hey Guni*, 'Guni' is the Creator, the ultimate maestro who creates magic with his song, which is a metaphor for life here. His song symbolises every aspect of this creation.

In the essay 'Sravansandhya', Gurudev writes (and we translate):

> This earth, the ocean, the sky—they all strive to emphatically express themselves; however there is no appropriate medium of expression but for a melodious tune—a tune in water-springs, a tune in the ecstatic spring air, a tune in the autumn blue sky… and that tune manifests itself not via spoken words but through its presence in music and painting. Hence, when nature wants to converse with us, it does so by arousing the sublime music that is embedded in our hearts. Word belongs to man, but song belongs to nature. Words are clear and constrained by context,

while songs are diffused and in anxious need for enmeshing into the endless. That is why it is through words that man makes contact with civilisation whereas songs enable man to connect with the universe. When man lends tune to a word that word outgrows its meaning and intertwines itself with the deep blue sky above—the tune goads man to make his happiness and grief a part of this universe; his pathos blend into the colour of dawn and dusk, and attain great charm by adjoining with the unspoken muse of this world—music helps man to be oblivious to the narrow mindedness of his daily life.

In one song he says:

Gaaner bhitor diye jokohon dekhi bhubonkhaani
Tokhon taare chini aami, tokhon taare jaani
(When I discover the universe through music
I see it deeply, I know it fully)

Music is omnipresent in all cosmic thoughts of Tagore. His mind was stirred by the same deep questions that trouble scientists, in order to unravel the mystery of creation through the aid of theory and experiments. Thus every entity—sun, moon, planet, man or tree—as felt by the Poet through a combination of spiritualism and science is expressed through his songs.

Mohaa bishhe, mohaakaashe, mohaa aalok maajhe,
Aami maanob, ekaaki bhromi, bishhoye brhomi bishhoye
(In the midst of the great universe, the vast sky, the spectacular light, I travel, lonesome and in amazement)

OR

Alo amar aalo ogo aaloy bhuban bhara
(My light, dear light that encompass the universe)

In the preface to Visva-Parichay, Gurudev writes to Satyandra Nath Bose:

> There is no ignominy in popularizing science through the aid of literature. This is why I have ventured to write on sciences, though I feel accountable, not just to literati, but to scientists as well, because science is unforgiving to inaccurate descriptions. I have therefore tried to be cautions despite my limitations. The fact is, I have felt duty-bound to write about science, not simply for students but for self as well. I have been able to educate myself through the writing of *Visva Parichay.* I feel such a pupil-like mentality may actually be useful for students at large.
>
> Needless to say I am not a serious student of science but I had this endless temptation to taste the juice of science from the very childhood. I was about nine or ten when I was introduced to Mr Sitanath Datta who used to frequent us every Sunday. I used to feel astonished when Mr Datta would explain certain standard theories of science through examples. I recall with amazement how he demonstrated by sprinkling saw dust—the phenomenon of convection—by hot water at the bottom of a vessel, put an fire, moving upwards, thereby causing colder water from the top move downwards.

The dialogue between Gurudev Tagore and the great physicist Albert Einstein touched upon the deeper meaning of the then-emerging subject of quantum mechanics. We quote from *Visva Parichay* again:

> …A physical macro object like a lump of stone or iron appears static from outside—as though they are epitome of motionlessness. However, it has been proven that molecules and atoms which constitute these bodies, are so miniscule that we cannot see them by normal means. But they are forever in a state of vibration. They vibrate when they are hot, they also vibrate when they are cold—only the degree of vibration varies.

> Indeed, more vigorous the vibration is, hotter is the object, as is felt by our senses. As we keep heating iron for instance, the constituent atoms get so unsettled that their excitement cannot be hidden. The vibrations accompanying the excitement that send waves through our nerves are what is referred to as heat wave. Indeed, heat hits us—light hits eyes, heat hits our body…
>
> *Bipul torongo re bipul torongo re*
> *Shob gogon udbelia—mogon kori oteet onagoto*
> (These enormous waves, these vast waves, are stirred by the vast sky, drowning the receding past)

Next comes the discussion of the atomic world, for which we translate from *Visva Parichay*:

> … The description is somewhat like this. If we continue to tear into pieces a mud house we are left with dust. When we cannot further pulverise the dust we feel we have reached to the basic constituent of the mud house. Similarly, physicists thought that when the worldly objects are reduced to a stage when they cannot be further subdivided we reach the atomic world. Atoms are so minute that ten crores of atoms make a line of one inch! We cannot of course break dust by simple means, but physicists have found ways of even breaking open the seemingly impregnable doors of atoms. When the latter are ripped apart, we obtain sub-atoms—namely electrons and protons. In order to give an idea of the size we are talking about, a renowned Astronomer has said, 'the space within the atom in which the electrons move about is like an emptied Howrah station in which five or six wasps are let loose.' But, what constrains these electrons within the vast empty space of atoms is the mass concentrated at the atomic centre that is the nucleus. Otherwise the atoms would not have existed, neither would the world we live in ….

We now know that the elliptical path the electron follows is not just one but multiple. These orbits are at definite distances from the centre, i.e., the nucleus. The electron cannot come closer to the nucleus than the nearest orbit from the nucleus. It can, however, transit from one orbit to another, apparently without any predetermined reason. The electron can absorb radiation to jump from an inner to an outer orbit, just as it can emanate radiation when it transits from an outer to an inner orbit. It is this emitted radiation that we call light. As long as the electron is constrained to move in the same orbit, there is no emission of light. This theory is one of the basics of quantum mechanics that explain why an atom retains its structure—why the universe remains intact.

Nrittyer boshe shundor holo bidrohi poromanu
(The rebellious atom retains integrity under the influence of waves)

In *Visva Parichay* we find allusions to gravitation and electromagnetism:

…It is speculated that more than a billion years ago something unusual had happened. A gigantic star had come close to the sun. The immense gravitational pull between this visiting star and the sun triggered waves of superheated gas. The gas further splintered into individual lumps of masses, some of which were gobbled up by the star, the rest began circulating around the sun. It is from these burning vapour balls emanated the planets, one of which is our mother earth. Because the splintered objects were relatively small in size, they cooled off faster. First, the gas liquefied and eventually became colder to form solid masses, such as the earth…

The universe that arose from the interplay of oppositely charged particles is characterised by contrasting forces leading to association and dissociation, attraction and repulsion, binding

> and unbinding. On the one hand, there is this great freedom—asymptotic freedom, in today's parlance—and on the other, there is this great attraction. Every object is either in a free state of motion or a bound state of attraction. The particulate matter in today's science is believed to be in a microscopic, miniscule form that is endowed with this dual property. Both properties are essential for the stability of the atom, just as they are for the structure of the universe. Millions of miles of emptiness separate the sun and the planets of our Solar System, yet the underlying gravitational pull has the invisible effect of making the planets revolve in their orbits, much like reined-in circus horses. Concomitantly, the sun also rotates within the galaxy of stars due to the same gravitational force, albeit much more slowly in relation to the earth. It is interesting to note that the space available to a planet in the solar system, relative to its size, is in the same ball park as the relative space available to an electron inside an atom. Therefore, just as planets orbit around the sun because of gravitational attraction, electrons rotate about the nucleus due to electromagnetic attraction. The difference is that, in contrast to gravity, unlike electric charges attract, like electric charges repel. The attempt to arrive at a 'Grand Unification' to put gravity on the same keel as other fundamental forces, including electromagnetic, has remained unsuccessful to date.

Rabindranath was also deeply concerned about the environment. His concern is very timely in view of the all-round degradation of the 'khoai' area, marked by remnants of the receding Kopai river, in the neighbourhood of Santiniketan. On the issue of climate, Tagore's writing in *Visva Parichay* translates thus:

> As the earth began the process of freezing into a solid lump from a liquid mass at the time of its inception its surroundings

were filled with humid vapour and carbon-related gases. Further cooling led to nitrogen and other gases. It is surprising at first sight that so much oxygen had survived even though the latter is highly reactant and prone to form compounds. The reason is—the abundance of trees and vegetation. The trees help imbibe carbon from atmospheric carbon dioxide to form cells and release oxygen. The resultant loss of carbon di-oxide is replenished from the exhaled air of living and non-living ones. It is surmised that life began from the semblance of oxygen left behind in ancient vegetation. The growth of the latter released further oxygen gas in the atmosphere at the expense of carbon di-oxide.

The molecule called chlorophyll is present in green leaves, which store sunlight in the form of energy. This energy helps create food in the form of fruits, crops, etc. On the other hand, the tiny amount of carbon-di-oxide in the air penetrates as carbon in vegetables, from which coal is produced, thereby aiding sustenance of life. It is the tree that is central to food production in the form of rice and wheat through the process of mixing carbon dioxide with water with the aid of chlorophyll, which draws energy from the sunlight.

Tagore captured the critical and essential importance of trees, plants, vegetation and crops in the evolution of man by institutionalising in Visva-Bharati certain festivities such as 'Briksha-ropan' (tree planting):

Morubijoyer keton udao shunne, hey probol praan
Dhulire dhonno koro korunar punne, hey komol praan
(Let the victory flag symbolising the conquering of the arid desert land flutter in the open-sky, ushering-in indomitable life – yet, it bless the earth with compassion, touching the delicate life)

And 'Halakarshan' (ploughing):

Aamra chash kori anonde
Mathe mathe bela kaate shokaal hothe shondhhe
(We plough our land in happiness; days get spent in the fields, from mornings to evenings)

We know quite a lot about the structure and atmosphere of our Mother Earth, though our knowledge about other planets is scanty. From the early days of its evolution, from a gaseous state into solid form, the Earth has undergone various metamorphoses. The evolutionary process of the Earth has left many imprints, especially on its outer surface, as the latter underwent the cooling cycle first. It is like this: When boiled milk is allowed to cool, its outer fatty layer forms a crinkled exterior. While we do not attach great importance to this phenomenon, the enormity of the size of the earth and the inability of the soft layer below to withstand the pressure of the crumpled top lead to severe contortions, yielding structures such as hills and mountains.

In addition to mountains, the stresses on the puckered surface of the earth also created gigantic craters. When these craters got filled-up with water, as a result of condensation of water-vapour in the earth's atmosphere during its cooling process, it led to oceans and seas. Furthermore, the water gets absorbed in the earth, gets vaporised and adds to rain clouds, which then replenish water bodies.

Maatir buker maajhe bondi je jol miliye thaake
Maati pai na, pai na, maati pai na taake
(Water, trapped deep under the earth is however denied to the soil)

We have been unable to dig as much into the earth's interior to unravel its structure. It is only a mile below the outer layer that has yielded coal mines. However, we do know

> that the deeper we probe, the hotter the composition is. The increase in temperature is not uniform, though. The present understanding is that there exists nearly two miles of a layer of iron and nickel, which have been created from the complex convection of heat currents through the materials of the Earth.

Iron is indeed the most important ore. It is given its due place in the festival 'Silpotsav', which we celebrate every year in Sriniketan.

> *Kothin loha kothin ghume chilo ocheton, o tar ghum bhangainu re*
> *Lokhho juger ondhokare chilo shongopone, ogo, tai, jagainu re*
> (The rigid iron ore remained a sleepy, lifeless lump, let us awaken it to application; it remained hidden in darkness through millions of years, let us stir it from its slumber)

A very powerful song indeed, and equally applicable symbolically to man's sloth and laziness. Today we know how the induction of carbon and nitrogen in iron converts it to steel, from which technology and industrialisation have flourished. Thus our own creative energy is also often entrapped in our slumber. The event of 'Shilpotsav' is a reminder of how we can overcome inertia by stoking our inner energy, like a piece of iron is energised into dynamism.

There is another area that has remained scientifically unexplored and undiscovered—the interface of science and philosophy. About this, the Poet's son Rathindranath has written in *Prantattwa*, which is translated here:

> We know, car engines have to be fed petrol that provides energy to help rotate the wheels. The same process applies to animals. The latter are able to function from the derived energy by burning food-intakes with oxygen. The burnt fuel is emitted by motors through their exhaust pipes; we too have various forms of excreting the discarded food items. From this

> point of view it is apt to draw a comparison between animals and machines. The crucial difference however is: Man has not been able to create a super machine like the human body. The characteristic feature of the latter is its ability to self-correct its mechanisms when they go wrong. The machines however do not possess this skill—they need engineers to fix them. A segment of scientists had once harboured the fallacious notion that every animal is like a machine. Humanists, philosophers and theologists, on the other hand, are aware of the supernatural power that a man is endowed with. This life-energy, what Bergson had called 'elan vital', must be appreciated in order to comprehend complex life processes.

Admittedly, many physiological activities are mechanics-driven, and may even be understood on the basis of chemical and electromagnetic methods; yet no current laboratory device can measure our thoughts and emotions. The unfathomable and profound mysteries of cognition can never be explained by the laws of mechanics, just as the latter do not account for the processes of procreation, upbringing, and transformation of humans.

In the earlier mentioned essay 'Srabansondhya', Gurudev had written and we translate:

> Man has an intriguing relation with nature. Nature manifests differently in the external world and in the inner soul of man. Take for example, a flower. No matter how elegant it looks, it seems to have arrived in the earth on a call of duty. The attire of the flower appears to be like that of a uniformed office-going employee—its mandate is to yield fruits; otherwise trees would not survive, world would turn into deserts. That is why flowers are endowed with colour and fragrance. As soon as the buds are pollinated by bees the flowers get busy to shed the leaf-cover, to dissipate the attractive scent. They seem to have no time other

> than the work assigned to them by nature. In this venture, the bud busily transits to flower, the flower to fruit, the fruit to seed, and the seed to tree—in this journey of evolution. A failure to perform this 'duty' of nature mercilessly causes the tree to shed the flower…
>
> It is the same flower, however, that finds complete leisure when it enters the domain of human perception and soul. It serves the dual purpose of an active worker in the external field of nature and of the epitome of peace and beauty within the inner self of man. Science says: 'No, you are wrong; the only purpose of a flower is to perpetuate the cycle of nature. You are needlessly connecting it to your aesthetic senses.' But our heart says: 'There has been no illusion. Just as the flower knocks on our doors as a captive labourer it manifests at the same time as a symbol of freedom. How can we accept one form as true and the other not?'

The genius of Tagore was multidimensional and holistic. He taught us to view our entire existence within an all-encompassing, coherent and undivided whole. There are numerous metaphors and allegories in his songs apparently presenting an idea, even while talking about something else. For instance, though the song *Tumi Ki Kebali Chhobi* was written with Kadambari Debi in mind, the same song was used by the Bard in *Sapmochon*; and the same song has scientific connotations:

> *Ooi je shudhur niharika, jara kore aache bheer,*
> *Ooi jara dinoratri aalo haathe choliyaache aandharer jaatri groho, tara, robi*
> (Glory to the milky way crowding the distant sky; glory to the passengers of darkness, carrying the lamp in their hands, day and night—planets, stars, sun)

Before concluding, we want to paraphrase in English a fascinating paragraph from Rathindranath's *Prantattwa*, related to our discussion above:

Rabindranath Tagore with Pratima and Rathindranath

There is one barrier to our understanding of the mystery of life. We who belong to the animal class are unable to traverse across our physical world. That world blinkers our view and judgment, because we can only measure those attributes that respond to our sensory organs. It is unrealistic therefore to find the ultimate answer through science of what life and soul are. In this case, the protagonist, i.e. the scientist himself is the judge making the issue one of 'conflict of interest', as the poser and responder are one and the same, as far as the fundamental query is concerned.

Bose, Mahalanobis and Tagore: Confluence of Minds

Jagadish Chandra Bose and Tagore were contemporaries—being just two and a half years apart in age—and indeed very good friends. However, Mahalanobis was more than 32 years younger than Tagore In fact, Mahalanobis was even younger than Rathindranath, Tagore's son. By the time he went to Cambridge for the Mathematical Tripos course, Tagore had already established himself as a great Poet, about to be awarded the Nobel Prize. So where was the confluence in terms of career, work and other attributes?

At the outset it is well to recognise that both J.C. Bose and Prasanta Chandra Mahalanobis were professional scientists. Bose is arguably our greatest scientist in physics and biology, while Mahalanobis is our tallest figure in statistics. It is curious, then, to analyse how Tagore, who was not a trained scientist, moved towards these two individuals who were vastly different from him. Most people who were close to Tagore were either followers or writers who propagated Tagore's views and became known as 'Rabindriks'. The exception perhaps was another great mathematical physicist, Satyendra Nath Bose. The reason seems easy to grasp: Tagore, being a colossal creator of ideas himself, was closely and inevitably drawn to other creative minds, albeit in distinct fields. This probably is one of the answers to my earlier query.

There was another point of confluence in that all of them were born in well-to-do Brahmo families. None had to struggle to make ends meet and all had been further enriched by their liberal, emancipated environments, which were imbued with culture, music and intellectual discourses. Not having to worry about money enabled them to be fiercely independent individuals who chartered their own paths in life, undeterred by distractions. There is one difference, however: Tagore never worked for anybody else; Bose did, albeit briefly, when he taught in Presidency College, administered by the British, and Mahalanobis worked very closely with the Government of India.

There was a particularly deep bond that existed between Tagore and Mahalanobis, who was attracted by the Poet's universalism. Though he, along with Sukumar Roy, initially met with resistance in getting Tagore inducted into the 'Sadharan Brahmo Samaj', he persisted with a logical chronicle on '*Keno Rabindranathke Chai*?'

Rabindranath Tagore with Jagadish Chandra Bose

Tagore was present during Mahalanobis's marriage to Nirmalkumari, more famously known as Rani, at his maternal uncle Shri Nilratan Sircar's home in 1923, marked by the absence of her own father, the legendary professor Heramba Chandra Maitra. Mahalanobis's close association with Tagore started when he came to Santiniketan in 1910 and later became one of the ten founder members of the 'Ashramik Sangha', what we call Alumni Association today. Mahalanobis became one of the two secretaries of Visva-Bharati, the other being Rathindranath, when it was established in 1921. He not only drafted the constitution of Visva-Bharati but remained its secretary until 1931 when the Indian Statistical Institute (ISI) was born.

In a series of articles in Bengali under the title *Rabindra Parichay*, published in 1922, in the leading monthly literary magazine *Prabasi*, Mahalanobis made a detailed study of Tagore's literary works. Tagore remained a close friend and stayed with Mahalanobis and Rani, on many occasions in their home, named by the Poet 'Amrapali'. It is interesting to note that it is Mahalanobis's father Prabodh Chandra who had helped record the voice of Tagore in 1924, when 28 songs and recitations were cut on the same day through a gramophone company called 'Carr and Mahalanobis', which the family owned. Amongst Mahalanobis's unpublished manuscripts, one finds an essay called 'Impact of Tagore on Modern India', in which he traces the roots of Tagore's philosophy to Indian heritage and concludes: 'I am fortunate indeed to have seen in the light of his face, his firm faith in the glory of Man.'

Another point of confluence of these three stalwarts lay in nation building—in creating and maintaining institutions, a faculty that is sadly lacking in present-day Bengal. Tagore's gigantic efforts in building this university—from the small step of creating a school with a handful of disciples in 1901, to establishing a university called Visva-Bharati in 1921—cannot be undermined. This was to be a special and unique university imparting holistic, humanistic and all-around education and research, rooted in its schools, Patha-Bhavana in Santiniketan and Siksha-Satra in Sriniketan. Teaching is still carried out in the midst of nature and the students are encouraged to imbibe a deep sense of culture through an exposure to music, dance, drama, rural reconstruction, cottage industry, and so on, before they graduate to higher and specialised learning.

Bose had made a similar contribution to institution building when he founded the Basu Bijnan Mandir, which was named the Bose Institute in 1917. What started with three departments of physics, botany and chemistry has blossomed into a full-fledged research institute comprising

Rabindranath Tagore with Prasanta Chandra Mahalanobis and his wife Nirmal Kumari

modern fields of biochemistry, microbiology, biophysics, cellular genetics, environmental science, nanotechnology, and radio and atmospheric sciences. The institute now is fully funded by the Department of Science and Technology of the Government of India.

Mahalanobis left mathematics and physics and turned his attention to statistics, then a budding field. As a matter of fact he pioneered the area of statistics and made seminal contributions to the subject. He made early inroads into the application of statistics to agriculture and interestingly, the first set of experiments was carried out in Sriniketan. Thus the genesis of support received today by Palli Siksha Bhavana from the Indian Council of Agriculture Research was sown back in 1924. The Indian Statistical Institute was established in 1931 with P.C. Mahalanobis appointed as the first Honorary Secretary. In 1950, when Mahalanobis was elected the General President of the Science Congress, his presidential speech was titled 'Why Statistics?' He professed, 'Statistics is an integral part of the dynamics of national planning. I hope this is a proper answer to the question: Why Statistics?'

Mahalanobis ended up as a close adviser to our first Prime Minister, Pandit Jawaharlal Nehru, and was the architect of the 5-year planning process. Today the Indian Statistical Institute (ISI) is a leading institution in the country with excellent teaching programmes involving B. Stat., M. Stat., B. Maths., etc., in addition to carrying out research in frontier areas.

The three great sons of India, Tagore, Bose and Mahalanobis, were all bonded together in their cherished dream of creating institutions for the nation free from the influence of our imperial masters. The endeavour of these three intellectuals can be seen as a significant contribution to the freedom movement. Though they were spurred by rationalism and the fervour of patriotic feelings, all of them realised that knowledge and education transcended national boundaries. They travelled abroad extensively and opened the door of their institutions to outsiders. In this effort, Mahalanobis perhaps stands the tallest. He had a plethora of very eminent scientists, statisticians and planners who spent time at the Indian

Statistical Institute (ISI). Some famous names are: Norbert Wiener, J.B.S. Haldane, Helen Spurway, Ronald Fisher, A.N. Kolmogorov, Abraham Wald, Oskar Lange, J.L. Doob, John K. Galbraith, P.M.S. Blackett, Frederic and Irene Julio Curie, Paul A.M. Dirac, and Niels Bohr. Tagore, Bose and Mahalanobis realised that the institutions they created must have their own publication houses, to strengthen independent intellectual discourses. We all know of our own Granthana-Vibhaga and its myriad publications. Bose, following the lead of the Royal Society (London) established an annual science journal named *Transaction of the Bose Research Institute*. To Mahalanobis's credit, the journal of statistics that he started in 1933, called *Sankhya* continues to remain a leading journal of statistics and is accessed and referred to by statisticians from all over the world.

Rabindranath Tagore and J.C. Bose—Two Soul-mates of the Cosmos

It is curious to analyse how Tagore, not a trained scientist, gravitated so close to Bose, one of our greatest scientists in the realm of physics and biology. Tagore was, of course, deeply interested in science, as can be substantiated by his discourses in *Visva Parichay*, and he is known to have rued the fact that he was never a student of science. Both these giants were also steeped in 'Upanishadic' thoughts that shaped their intellectual pursuit.

Tagore has written about Bose:

> '…[T]o my mind Bose appeared to be the poet of the world of facts that waited to be proved…,whereas my own world of visions had their value…, because a part of my nature is logical which not only enjoys making playthings of facts, but seeks pleasure in an analytical view of objective reality…'

In another letter to Bose, Tagore mentioned:

> I have expressed by inner feelings in a poem for you…It is my privilege that I have you as a friend; I have acknowledged that pride more firmly through the cadence of a poem—In the coming years memories of you will be entwined with mine—that is my greatest joy…

A poem Tagore wrote for Bose in the year 1928 reads thus:

> *Mone aachhe ekoda jedin*
> *Ashonno prochhonno tobo, osrudhar, ondhokaare leen*

The English transcription of which is:

> I remember the day when your moistened eyes were hidden in darkness, and you were treading the envy-ridden path with hurt feet, and you were exhausted by the incessantly meaningless battle with small-minded hostility. It is that grief which would remain your companion, it is that fire which would alight your road, it is that indifference which would fortify your inner self. Today your reputation is heard all over, your fame has spread across the shores of ocean; my friend – you are radiant by your own inner light- your vast contribution is embodied in your works. Today a thousand lamps have lit the festival of light in the galaxy of stars wherein you have found a place. Allow me to add to this my own solitary lamp which you might view as the lamp of your friend; it is your lone poet friend who had come to garland you when you were throttled by hindrances from all sides; he did not have to await the public nod to come forward with offerings in your days of hardship. Today, your dear friend is delighted to join the chorus of thousand voices to pronounce: Glory to you, Glory to your coworkers, glory to your holy mother land.

Tagore would often invite Bose to Silaidaha. Bose accepted the invitation with the condition that Tagore would have to tell him a new story every day. It was good for Tagore to accept the condition, as he relished writing and narrating to Bose a new story every evening. Incidentally, Bose, the 'Poet of the World', himself wrote eloquently in Bengali. During one such get-together in Silaidaha, Tagore composed the famous poem 'Karna-

Kunti Sambad', in which the character of Karna was designed by the Poet at the behest of his scientist friend.

Bose on his part published some of Tagore's works in English during his jaunts to Europe and the US during 1908–09. The first attempt at publishing 'Kabuliwala' failed when Harper said they were not interested in a tale of an Indian native, but Bose persisted and finally succeeded in 1914–15 in publishing this story from the US.

As mentioned earlier, both the stalwarts had contributed towards institution building. Basu Bijnan Mandir, founded in 1917 and now known as the Bose Institute, followed a curious turn of events. Bose had received a show-cause notice by the Principal of Presidency College for showing the famous physicist Lord Rayleigh around his laboratory without the Principal's prior permission. Bose felt insulted and decided to establish his own lab. He had discussed his plan way back in 1898 with Tagore, who promised financial help but it took almost 20 years before the plan fructified. Remarkable words were uttered by Bose at the inception:

> It is not only a research laboratory, but also a Temple. Broadly, we know that science tries to reveal the truth by cognition, and the instruments widen that cognition. There are certain truths, which exist outside the domain of scientific methods and which can be acquired solely by faith and belief. That is the main reason for establishing such a Temple because, it is the most befitting place for perceiving that faith-influenced truth. This institute will sow the seed of such specified belief and conviction, which will open the door for fulfilling the greater demand and to convert the impossible into possible in future.

The management committee included Tagore, amongst other members. Tagore, along with Sir Nilratan Sircar, also figured in the Regulating Committee of the institution. The lecture hall at the entrance of the institute had walls adorned by Nandalal Bose's paintings. Tagore had composed the invocation, 'Matrimandira punnya angana' for the inauguration, which, like 'Amader Santiniketan', is sung on every Foundation Day and other special functions. Tagore had helped raise funds through generous support from kings, zamindars, and businessmen, and remarked in his memorial lecture:

> Jagadish succeeded in bringing Lakshmi in his own favour so easily only due to his personal magnetism.

The degree of deep attachment and bonding between the two can be assessed from the letters Tagore wrote to Bose, documented in *Chithipatra* Vol. 6. These letters describe the remarkable synergy and symbiosis between these two extraordinary individuals. The letters are full of wit, deep affection and tongue-in-cheek remarks, characteristic of Tagore. What is to be noted is the gradual change in the modes of address Tagore used and how he signed off, in these letters.

> **26 May 1899**
> **Calcutta**
> Dear Sir,
> Suddenly there are untimely rains in Calcutta. I am not complaining but I fear, lest Nature gives 'Sraban' a miss! I do not envy your good fortune if it is raining in Darjeeling too. Rains in the hills are monotonous and incessant, like the wailing and tears of Bengalis…
> Yours,
> Rabindranath Tagore

> **17 September 1900**
> **Silaidaha**
> **Kumarkhali,**
> **Nadia**

Dear Friend,

I was browsing through a book on French grammar—suddenly your letter stirred me as though a dead frog had been enlivened by an electric current.

...Do announce war—don't spare anybody—victory will come, upon which we Bengalis will enjoy the spoils of your glory. We do not have to understand the depth of your scientific work—what suffices is what the *London Times* writes! All we would like to do would be to latch on to the glorious appreciation emanating from the Englishmen. Then some famous newspapers of our country would write 'We are no less than anybody else.' Some other paper would write, 'We are on the path of newer scientific discoveries.' Nobody here actually cares for you; however, you are ours only when you win the kudos of the world. The labour of harvesting is yours—but the benefits must befall us. Thus, when you are victorious, victory will be ours...

Yours,

Rabindranath Tagore

October / November 1900

Friend,

Can the boat which the Caesar rides in, capsize? Great work has found refuge in thy self—therefore, you must get well soon.

...I give all your news to the Maharaja of Tripura. I am very pleased to notice his high regards for you. He has sent a message that he is ready to help with more than he had promised earlier.

What have you decided about your assignment in England? I have already given you my opinion—do not hesitate a bit. You may have to bid adieu to your own country if that stands in the way of your success...

Rabindranath Tagore

20 November 1900

Calcutta

Friend,

...The Maharaja of Tripura is now in Calcutta. I can't describe how genuinely happy he feels at your scientific success. He has specially touched my heart because he has so much heartfelt admiration for you. He will be pleased when I would show him your letter. His glee was perceptive when he had recently received your letter—as though he had been specially honoured. He seems extremely keen to help you in any way he can.

...Just met the Maharaja. He was very happy to read your letter. Listen, can we not make you independent if you would rather carry out your research from this country? Shame on us if we cannot compensate you for the meagre salary you earn in your job. But, would you really accept our proposal? How can you work freely when you are hassled all the time and shackled from all sides? We wish to free you—I do not think that it will be difficult. What do you say?

Yours,

Rabindranath Tagore

12 December 1900

Friend,

...Are you not entitled to leave without pay if the Government does not grant you study leave? We can make a special effort to make up your loss if that possibility exists. Do not come back with unfinished work. I will take the responsibility of supporting you monetarily but please do not neglect your work. I am not sure how much I will make from the translation of my works—I want to make you avail of the entire proceeds...

Yours,

Rabindranath Tagore

January 1901

Friend,

I cannot get over the fear that your mission will be incomplete if you would make an untimely return to India. You must accomplish your objectives even if that would mean sacrifice. The whole world must be exposed to the vibrations and waves that are traveling like scientific light through your head. Our interest coincides with your work—it is us who must bear all the expenses for the fulfilment of your assignment. Please do not make a premature return—this is my humble advice.

…I wish the new century will be enlightened by the wisdom of your new discovery"

Yours, Rabindranath Tagore

May 1901

Friend,

…Bela's marriage has been fixed this month. …It is my misfortune that my friends will not be present—you are in England, Loken likewise, Maharaj is perhaps in Agartala, Natore in the Nilgiris…can you not create a wireless electricity vehicle through which you can illuminate your friend's festival with your divine smile ? Do send your blessings for the newly-wed.

I want to give you an assignment. You will have to select a good tutor from England for the Prince (of Tripura)…The tutor ought to be a man of science…Of course, there is every reason to assume that your selected man will turn useless, thanks to the virtues of the Indian environment! However, Maharaj will not blame you for that…

Yours,

Rabindranath Tagore

3 July 1901

Friend,

...Your present for Bela has been much appreciated... My son-in-law has turned out to be much likeable—not like the usual Bengali lads. He is polite and humble, but of strong character—is outstanding in studies and intellectual pursuits; one other quality I saw in him—he has liked Bela!

...I gathered courage in writing an essay in the Sraban issue of *Bongadarshan* about your new discovery, with the aid of some data from an electricity expert. First I thought I would ask Jagadananda. But I did not like what he wrote. There are possibilities of errors which will perhaps amuse you. ...The indication that I provided in the Ashad issue of Bongadarsan was not scientifically correct—I could not find an electricity expert at that time! ...Can you find ways of traveling to Germany and America? If you stay long in Europe, I'll definitely make an attempt to call on you.

Yours,

Rabindranath Tagore

There are many such letters in *Chhithipatra,* Vol.6, but here is an excerpt from what Tagore had quoted from Bose's own statement on his discovery.

I have shown you this evening the autographic records of the history of stress and strain in both the living and non-living. How similar are the two sets of writings, so similar indeed that you cannot tell them one from the other! They show you the waxing and waning pulsations of life—the climax due to stimulants, the gradual decline of fatigue, the rapid setting in of death-rigor from the toxic effect of poison.

It was when I came on this mute witness of life and saw an all-pervading unity that binds together all things—the mote that thrills on ripples of light, the teeming life on earth and the radiant suns that shine on it—it was then that for the first time I understood the message proclaimed by my ancestors on the banks of the Ganges thirty centuries ago—'They who behold the One, in all the changing manifoldness of the universe, unto them belongs eternal truth, unto none else, unto none else.'

Here are a couple of letters from Tagore to Bose that demonstrate his appreciation for Bose's work on plant science, which are marked by his characteristic humour.

21 May 1901 Silaidaha

Friend,

…I feel proud to read about the method you have discovered to pinch every aspect of nature. Until now, inanimate objects were troubling us—now I can contemplate revenge on them, thanks to your discovery. Go ahead and administer un-ending pinches and poisons to them—don't leave them alone. From now on, Judges can pronounce 'Pinching Punishments' for inanimate objects if they ever come up for courtroom trials…

Do get prepared for an extended stay in England for the sake of your work. Do not spoil your endeavour by returning in the midst of the troubles here. Please do not hesitate to write me in detail how much money you will need for this extended sojourn.

Yours,

Rabindranath Tagore

4 June 1901

Friend,

Bravo—glories to you. I am in cloud nine since this morning after receiving your letter. I have lowered myself to the feet of the Almighty who, through your work, has erased the shame of our country….

My friend, please accept my offerings, for which my heart feels so keen. Glory to you—please ignite the lamp of knowledge of my India as its new Sage…

Once again I plead– do not make an untimely return to India. Please complete your penance—you are the one who would rescue Sita from the 'Asokyan'…I can bask in the reflected glory of my country if I can be of small help in this cause…My deep regret is that I am not with you to shake your hands at these times of your glorious achievements…

Yours,
Rabindranath Tagore

So what did Tagore think of Bose? In a tribute to him, Tagore wrote:

Years ago, when Bose, in his militant exuberance of youthfulness, was contemptuously defying all obstacles to the progress of his endeavour, I came into intimate contact with him, and became infected with his vigorous hopefulness. There was every chance of his frightening me away into a respectful distance, making me aware of the airy nothingness of my own imaginings. But to my relief, I found in him a dreamer, and it seemed to me, what surely was a half-truth, that it was more his magical instinct than the probing of his reason which startled out secrets of nature before sudden flashes of his imagination. In this I felt our mutual affinity but at the same time our difference, for to my mind he appeared to be the poet of the world of facts that waited to be proved by the scientist for their final triumph, whereas my own world of visions had their value, not in their absolute probability, but in their significance of delightfulness. All the same, I believe that a part of my nature is logical which not only enjoys making playthings of facts, but seeks pleasure in an analytical view of objective reality. I remember often having been assured by my friend that I only lacked the opportunity of training to be a scientist but not the temperament. Thus in the prime of my youth I was strangely attracted by the personality of this remarkable man and found his mind sensitively alert in the poetical atmosphere of enjoyment which belonged to me.

At this time he was busy detecting in the behaviour of the non-living some hidden impulses of life. This aroused a keen enthusiasm in me who had ever been familiar with the utterance of the Upanishada which proclaims that whatever there is in this moving world vibrates with life. Afterwards he shifted his enquiries from the field of physics to the biological realm of plants. With the marvellously sensitive instruments which he invented he magnified the inaudible whisperings of vegetable life, which seemed to him somewhat similar in language to the message of our own nerves. My mind was overcome with joy at the idea of the unity of the heart-beats of the universe, and I felt sure that the pulsating light which palpitates in the stars has its electric kinship in the life that throbs in my own veins. I knew that this was not science, but my mind trembled with the hope that the opening message had already been declared and final evidences were in preparation.

At last when Jagadish Chandra sailed across the sea to place the results of his researches before the questioning scrutiny of the West, my heart expanded with an undoubting expectation of our country's claim to a world-recognition being accepted and at the prospect of a wide establishment of a wonderful truth which is native to our oriental attitude of mind. With what little lay in my power I helped him in his adventure but, fortunately, since then, no more help was needed either in companionship or in other ways from a man like me who was too heavily burdened with his own responsibilities. His fame spread rapidly and material contributions from all sides showered upon his schemes, which centralised at last in the Bose Institute. I fervently hope that the Spirit of Science will find its lasting shrine in this place and the

> aspiration of the great master will remain a living force in its heart, making it a perpetual memorial worthy of him.
>
> This tribute of mine to the memory of Jagadish will appear inadequately feeble, especially in contrast to the repeated magnification of his name in my writings both in prose and verse at the time when his fame was not luminously apparent above the horizon and when, I am sure, my fellowship and unfaltering faith in his genius did hearten and help him. But my struggling health, which has lately been wrenched back from the grip of death, is incompetent for most of my important tasks, and also the singeing hope that began its first soaring in immensity, has completed its journey in its terminus.'

Here is another quote from the memorial address that Tagore delivered at the foundation of the Basu Bijnan Mandira:

> When by some fortunate chance I came into an intimate contact with Sir Jagadish, he was in the prime of his youth and I was very nearly of his age. At that moment his mind seemed entranced with a vision of the living creatures' fundamental kinship with the world of the unconscious. He was busy in employing his marvellous inventiveness in coaxing mute Nature to yield her hidden language. The response which he received through skilful questionings revealed to him glimpses of the mystery of an existence that concealed its meaning underneath a contradiction of its appearance. I had the rare privilege of sharing the daily delight of his constant surprises. I believe, poets inherit the primeval age in their temperament when things in their infant simplicity revealed a common feature. Somehow these lovers of Maya feel the joy of their being spread all over the creation, which makes them indulge in seeking the analogy of the living in things that appear lifeless. Such an attitude of mind may not in all cases be based upon any definite belief, animistic or

pantheistic; it may be merely a make-believe, as we notice in children's play, which owes its origin to the lurking tendency in our sub-conscious mind to ascribe life-energy to all activities in the natural world. I was made familiar from my boyhood with the Upanishada which, in its primitive intuition, proclaims that whatever there is in this world vibrates with life, the life that is one in the infinite…'

Rabindranath Tagore with Albert Einstein

Einstein–Tagore: A Discourse

Rabindranath Tagore (1861–1941) met with Albert Einstein (1879–1955) on five occasions, once in 1926 and four times in 1930. Two of their meetings were recorded. In 1930, Tagore was about seventy years of age, and was already in bad health. What made him travel all the way to Berlin? Was the reason a mere curiosity to chat with someone who, after having propounded the theories of Special Relativity (1905) and General Relativity (1915), had been anointed as a colossus, a cult figure of Western science?

My surmise is that Tagore's profound interest in science and its foundational issues, as well as what is called the philosophy of science, propelled him to ignore the travails of long travels, to interact with similar minds of Europe, not just Einstein but great thinkers like Romain Rolland (1861–1944), H. G. Wells (1866–1940), Sigmund Freud (1856–1939) and others. In 1930, Einstein was just above fifty, eighteen years younger than Tagore, and a Nobel Laureate of 1921, having given the theory of the photoelectric effect in 1905. As mentioned above, 1905 was also the year that saw the path-breaking formulation of relativity, not to mention the clearest exposition of a phenomenon called the Brownian motion, which had defied scientific explanation for close to eighty years. Such was the impact of the three papers of Einstein in 1905 on the Special Theory of Relativity, Brownian motion, and blackbody radiation (photoelectric effect) that the United Nations had decided to celebrate 2005 as the centenary of the 'Miraculous Year of Physics.'

I have already discussed in earlier sections Tagore's abiding fascination with science, in particular physical sciences, that goaded him to writing *Visva Parichay* in 1934, four years after meeting with Einstein. In fact, in *Visva Parichay*, Tagore had alluded to the photoelectric effect (cf. Section 2b) where he had wondered:

> …Though a far distance away stars…make their presence felt through light—some visible, some however invisible to the naked eye. Question then arose—what is the mode of travel of light? The answer is a fascinating story—light travels as waves. It is difficult to fathom the nature of this wave. Concomitantly however, another piece of data brought out a contrasting picture of light—that light consists of innumerable corpuscles or tiny particles…

The photoelectric effect was also, in a way, the genesis of Quantum Theory, which shook the world of physics. Until Einstein's work in 1905, the three monumental pillars of physics were (1) Johannes Kepler's (1571–1630) laws of planetary orbits, (2) Isaac Newton's (1643–1727) laws of mechanical motion and gravitation, and (3) James Clerk Maxwell's (1831–1879) equations of electrodynamics. Together they formed what is dubbed the Classical Theory of Physics which was perceived to be unconquerable frontiers. Classical physics had established that light travels as transverse waves—transverse because the direction of propagation is perpendicular to the two-dimensional plane of 'polarisation' of electric and magnetic fields that constitute light. The explanation of the photoelectric effect changed that perception—light is also composed of particulate objects called photons, a name that was curiously coined by one of the world's greatest physical chemists, Gilbert N. Lewis (1875–1946). Tagore had referred to this fascinating interplay, the 'wave-particle duality', in *Visva Parichay* (Section 2b), which we quote once more:

> How does one reconcile these two apparently contradictory picturisation of light? What is more mind-boggling is that while the external manifestation of light is either as a wave or a particle, what appears in the micro world is neither this nor that—we call it 'radiation'.

This duality was the cornerstone of the newly emerging quantum mechanics.

Ironically Einstein, having sown the seeds of Quantum Theory during his 1905 discourse on the Planck Theory of Radiation that paved the path for explaining the photoelectric effect, was philosophically opposed to the *probabilistic* interpretation of quantum mechanics. He had made this oft-quoted statement: 'God does not play dice with the universe!' The probabilistic interpretation (based on 'chance') meant that a fundamental particle like electron, discovered nine years ago (in 1896), cannot be said to be located in one definite position—one can only attribute a certain probability of finding the electron at a specific point in space. Also, the moment one tries to measure the (static) position of the electron its dynamics, measured by the momentum, become uncertain, thus bringing into fore the essential presence of the measuring apparatus—hitherto considered to be a bystander in the 'classical' interpretation of physics.

Tagore, on the other hand, was drawn to this aspect of 'duality' and the interaction between the measuring apparatus and the measured object because of, I reckon, his upbringing in deep 'Upanishadic' thoughts of Indian philosophy. Duality and measurement, the foundational principles of the Quantum Theory, are also recurring themes in our Eastern philosophy—the same human mind can simultaneously live in different spaces. The perception of an object as beautiful, or a phenomenon as true, is possible only through the observation (read: measurement) of the beholder, etc. These notions are deeply engrained doctrines of the Upanishads. Naturally, Tagore was stirred by these emerging, revolutionary concepts of the new developments in physics that resonated with what he believed as 'Atman', the self and its interaction with the Creator.

Given this background, I believe the dialogue between Einstein and Tagore ought to be viewed from the perspective of a 'meeting of minds' of two then-contemporary philosophers—one steeped into Eastern moorings and the other in rational Western ideas. Einstein was considered to be the most influential physicist of the 20th century. On the contrary, Tagore was not formally trained in physics but had a strong intuitive understanding (as well as basic knowledge) of mathematics—he used to indulge in that subject in-between writing poetry and novels! After all, his first serious writing was composed in his teens on astronomy.

Both Tagore and Einstein saw nature as the essential laboratory of science and therefore, both were phenomena-driven. Though Einstein is popularly viewed as a strong mathematical physicist—perhaps because of his extensive use of tensor algebra and curved-space geometry in the General Theory of Relativity—the 1905 Einstein was a down-to-earth physicist. The earlier mentioned contributions to Brownian motion and blackbody radiation were both inspired by natural phenomena, backed by experimental observations in the laboratory. The employed mathematics is simple, easily understandable today even by high school students. Even in formulating the Special Theory of Relativity, in which he had abandoned the notion of time being absolute, Einstein had employed 'gedanken' ('thought') experiments to simulate what it means to comprehend time as relative. Once again, it is the 'space-time symmetry', which broke away from the established classical notions and put time on equal footing as space, had fascinated Tagore. Therefore, it is not surprising that Rabindranath sought Einstein out in Berlin to bounce his own thoughts on Einstein, whom he held in the highest esteem.

On his part, Einstein showed tremendous respect for Tagore, as can be discerned in a letter in 1926 after they had jointly signed an anti-war 'Declaration of the Independence of the Spirit': 'If there is anything in Germany that you would like and which could be done by me, I beg you to command me at any time.' Then there was another letter to Tagore, written by Einstein's step-daughter Margot: 'At once, I ran to father with your letter to read to him; father loves you too, you know…' Both individuals had shown common concerns about humanity, truth and science. Morianoff,

Margot's husband, who was present in the Berlin meetings, had this to say: 'Tagore is the poet with the head of a thinker while Einstein is the thinker with the head of a poet.'

In apparent disregard of this personal equation between Tagore and Einstein, as alluded to above, several authors, mainly Western, have implied that the two of them talked past each other. Einstein was not conversant in English while Tagore was uncomfortable with German; Tagore was the 'mystic' of the East who was 'repetitive' while Einstein was a logical and systematic thinker of physics who based his work on mathematical reasoning. I do not subscribe to this simplistic view of the famous encounter. I believe both men were humanists and Universalists, both were tormented by the war-torn world and both transcended national boundaries to acquire the exulted status of gurus like Mahatma Gandhi (1869–1948), Bertrand Russel (1872–1970) and Leo Tolstoy (1852–1910). It is only a curious coincidence that Tagore and Einstein belonged to two ancient philosophies (that have many commonalities, in my view) of Indian and Jewish civilisations and Indo-German language-links. Both had minimal training in research—Einstein had been working as a technical assistant in a Swiss patent office when he was smitten by physics in his early twenties—and therefore, the creativity inherent in them was truly intrinsic and self-driven. Their personal bondage can be exemplified by the poem Tagore wrote for Einstein: 'The same sun is newly born in new lands in a ring of endless dawns.' (It is only a matter of inquisitive conjecture whether or not the referral to the 'sun' is actually to 'Robi', the Bengali word for sun, metaphorically speaking). The above mentioned ode is in gratitude to Einstein's contribution (along with J.C. Bose, Gandhi and Rolland) to *The Golden Book of Tagore*, a Festschrift in honour of Tagore's seventieth birthday. Prior to that, in 1930, before he had met with Einstein, Tagore had delivered the Hibbert Lectures at Oxford University, which were published in 1931 (along with the conversation with Einstein in Appendix) as *The Religion of Man.* In the latter, Tagore argued that the truth of the world lies in 'The human mind with all its limitations.' The supreme ideal was the spiritual man, rather than an external God.

One other red herring is the apparent mental partitioning of the Tagore-Einstein dialogue between two different segments: (1) science and philosophy and (2) music. In my opinion these attempts are facile. The discourse on music was not disjoint from science but a natural and smooth transition through which one gets an integrated glimpse of the unifying aspects of science and music. (It is only incidental that Einstein was an accomplished violinist.)

From time immemorial man has asked the questions: Why are we here? Where do you go from here? Who makes the sun and the moon rise and set regularly? How do we comprehend natural phenomena around us? While we understand how our body functions do we know how the mind that subsumes emotion, empathy, antipathy, etc., works?

Different people with different training approach these questions differently. Poets, novelists, musicians, and historians usually face these issues from the perspective of how the mind works. That is why they are said to belong to the field of humanities. Scientists, on the other hand, would like to view natural phenomena described by a logical structure that is provided by mathematics. The strength of mathematics lies in the fact that once the axioms are specified, the internal consistency of mathematical equations takes over—there is no room for fudging or multiple interpretations. Physicists, using mathematical modelling, like to think of every entity of creation as being guided by one of the four fundamental forces: (1) gravity, (2) electromagnetic, (3) strong and the concomitant (4) weak interactions. Gravitational forces, the weakest of the four, guide planetary motion, and play an essential role in modern cosmology. On the other hand, most of what we experience in the material world, be it in television pictures, cellphone talks, photosynthesis in trees and leaves, the colour of the sky, animals, flowers, etc. are governed by electro-magnetic forces. Finally, what goes on inside an atomic nucleus—within a proton or a neutron—is dictated by a combination of strong and weak forces.

Despite great advances made because of quantum theory and relativity, which have enabled us to comprehend electromagnetic and strong/weak forces from a unified mathematical framework a 'grand unification', bringing in gravity within the fold has eluded us so far. The modern developments in string theory are ongoing attempts in this direction.

The foregoing discussion underscores the propensity of physicists to explain everything about the universe from a unified point of view. Rabindranath Tagore, curiously enough, belonged to a class of extraordinary individuals who did not want to see knowledge as fragmented, but viewed everything about nature and the cosmos from a holistic perspective. For Tagore, science, humanities, music, and art all have a common goal to comprehend the truth.

Here is a recorded conversation between Rabindranath Tagore and Albert Einstein, from 14 July 1930, to bring a new perspective:

> Einstein: Do you believe in the Divine as isolated from the world? (*The Oxford Dictionary* states 'Divine' as derived from God but also gives its old-fashioned meaning as superhumanly beautiful, wonderful.)
> Tagore: Not isolated. The infinite personality of Man comprehends the universe. There cannot be anything that cannot be subsumed by the human personality, and this proves that the truth of the universe is human truth. I have taken a scientific fact to illustrate this—Matter is composed of protons, neutrons and electrons, with gaps between them; but matter may seem to be solid, with links between spaces which unify the individual subatomic particles. Similarly, humanity is composed of individuals, yet they have their inter-connection of human relationship, which gives living solidarity to Man's world. The entire universe is linked up with us in a similar manner, it is a human universe. I have pursued this thought through art, literature and the religious consciousness of man.

What we perceive in this material world—tables, chairs, cars, etc.—are macro objects, governed by classical laws. But every such object is made up of microscopic constituents such as molecules, atoms, electrons, so on, which obey quantum laws. Thus, according to Tagore, the construct of an object as a 'table' is only through our own perception. Also, the property of a table is very different from that of its microscopic components. An interesting analogy can be found in the music that Tagore created, called Rabindrasangit, in which he had assimilated components of Hindustani, Carnatic and even Western music. The point is that the final shape that Rabindrasangeet takes like the 'table' is a wholesome entity. In a similar view, it is futile to seek the individual property of hydrogen H (mostly perceived as gas), sulphur S (associated with powder) and oxygen O (again viewed as gas) in the compound H_2SO_4, which is sulphuric acid. Therefore, what is beautiful, or true or profound, is only in the human mind. This line of thought is further continued in the conversation of the duo:

> Einstein: There are two different conceptions about the nature of the universe: (1) The world as a unity dependent on human. (2) The world as a reality independent of the human factor.
>
> Tagore: When our universe is in harmony with Man, the eternal, we know it as truth, we feel it as beauty.
>
> Einstein: This is the purely human conception of the universe.
>
> Tagore: There can be no other conception. This world is a human world—the scientific view of it is also that of the scientific man. There is some standard of reason and enjoyment which gives it truth, the standard of the Eternal Man whose experiences are through our experiences.
>
> Einstein: This is a realisation of the human entity.
>
> Tagore: Yes, one eternal entity. We have to realise it through our emotions and activities. We realised the Supreme Man who has no individual limitations through our limitations. Science is concerned with that which is not confined to individuals; it is the impersonal human world of truths. Religion realises these truths and links them up with our deeper needs; our individual consciousness of truth gains universal significance. Religion applies values to truth, and we know this truth as good through our own harmony with it.
>
> Einstein: Truth, then, or beauty is not independent of Man?

> Tagore: No.
>
> Einstein: If there would be no human beings any more, the Apollo of Belvedere would no longer be beautiful.
>
> Tagore: No.
>
> Einstein: I agree with regard to this conception of beauty, but not with regard to truth.
>
> Tagore: Why not? Truth is realised through man.
>
> Einstein: I cannot prove that my conception is right, but that is my religion.

In the pronouncement, 'If there would be no human being any more, the Apollo of Belvedere would no longer be beautiful', we discern trace of the quantum-measurement process: the electron can have an 'up-spin' or a 'down-spin', but we will not know which, unless we make an observation or a measurement. The perception of beauty is also in the 'eyes of the beholder'. The physically deformed Aruneswar (in Tagore's musical called 'Sapmochan') transforms from ugly to beautiful as the state of mind of his lover Kamalika (wife in an earlier incarnation) changes.

> Tagore: Beauty is in the ideal of perfect harmony which is in the Universal Being; Truth is the perfect comprehension of the Universal Mind. We individuals approach it through our own mistakes and blunders, through our accumulated experiences, through our illumined consciousness—how, otherwise, can we know truth?
>
> Einstein: I cannot prove scientifically that truth must be conceived as a truth that is valid independent of humanity; but I believe it firmly. I believe, for instance, that the Pythagorean Theorem in geometry states something that is approximately true, independent of the existence of man. Anyway, if there is a reality independent of man, there is also a truth relative to this reality; and in the same way the negation of the first engenders a negation of the existence of the latter.

Tagore: Truth, which is one with the Universal Being, must essentially be human, otherwise whatever we individuals realise as true can never be called truth—at least the truth which is described as scientific and which only can be reached through the process of logic, in other words, by an organ of thoughts which is human. According to Indian philosophy there is Brahman, the absolute truth, which cannot be conceived by the isolation of the individual mind or described by words but can only be realised by completely merging the individual in its infinity. But such a truth cannot belong to science. The nature of truth which we are discussing is an appearance—that is to say, what appears to be true to the human mind and therefore is human, may be called *maya* or illusion.

Einstein: So according to your conception, which may be the Indian conception, it is not the illusion of the individual, but of humanity as a whole.

Tagore: The species also belong to a unity, to humanity. Therefore the entire human mind realises truth; the Indian or the European mind meet in a common realisation.

Einstein: The word species is used in German for all human beings, as a matter of fact, even the apes and the frogs would belong to it.

Tagore: In science we go through the discipline of eliminating the personal limitations of our individual minds and thus reach that comprehension of truth which is in the mind of the Universal Man.

Einstein: The problem begins whether truth is independent of our consciousness.

Tagore: What we call truth lies in the rational harmony between the subjective and objective aspects of reality, both of which belong to the super-personal man.

Einstein: Even in our everyday life we feel compelled to ascribe a reality independent of man to the objects we use. We do this to connect the experiences of our senses in a reasonable way. For instance, if nobody is in this house, yet that table remains where it is.

Tagore: Yes, it remains outside the individual mind, but not the universal mind. The table which I perceive is perceptible by the same kind of consciousness which I possess.

Einstein: If nobody would be in the house the table would exist all the same—but this is already illegitimate from your point of view—because we cannot explain what it means that the table is there, independently of us. Our natural point of view in regard to the existence of truth apart from humanity cannot be explained or proved, but it is a belief which nobody can lack—no primitive beings even. We attribute to truth a super-human objectivity; it is indispensable for us, this reality which is independent of our existence and our experience and our mind—though we cannot say what it means.

Tagore: Science has proved that the table as a solid object is an appearance and therefore that which the human mind perceives as a table would not exist if that mind were naught. At the same time it must be admitted that the fact, that the ultimate physical reality is nothing but a multitude of separate revolving centres of electric force, also belongs to the human mind. In the appreciation of truth there is an eternal conflict between the universal human mind and the same mind confined in the individual. The perpetual process of reconciliation is being carried on in our science, philosophy, in our ethics. In any case, if there be any truth absolutely unrelated to humanity then for us it is absolutely non-existing.

It is not difficult to imagine a mind to which the sequence of things happens not in space but only in time like the sequence of notes in music. For such a mind such conception of reality is akin to the musical reality in which Pythagorean geometry can have no meaning. There is the reality of paper, infinitely different

> from the reality of literature. For the kind of mind possessed by the moth which eats that paper literature is absolutely non-existent, yet to Man's mind, literature has a greater value of truth than the paper itself. In a similar manner if there be some truth which has no sensuous or rational relation to the human mind, it will ever remain as nothing so long as we remain human beings.
>
> Einstein: Then I am more religious than you are!
>
> Tagore: My religion is in the reconciliation of the Super-personal Man, the universal human spirit, in my own individual being.

At this point it is pertinent to understand determinism, causality and Quantum Theory, in the background of the Einstein-Tagore dialogue.

Imagine a cricket ball being hurled upwards with an initial velocity (speed) that may be denoted by v (*t=0*). The symbol *t=0* within the brackets indicates the zero of time *t*. Because the ball is pulled downwards by the earth's gravitational force, it would reach a terminal height and then fall down. Ignoring the friction in the surrounding air medium, the classical laws of motion state that the subsequent height of the ball, denoted by z (*t*), is completely determined in terms of z (*t=0*) and v (*t=0*). This, in simple terms, is the meaning of classical determinism. It is also a statement of causality: The cause is {z (*t=0*), v (*t=0*)} while the effect is z (*t*). The cause must precede the effect.

On the other hand, instead of the cricket ball, if a fundamental particle like an electron (or even a hydrogen atom) is injected upwards, neither its height z (*t*) nor its velocity v (*t*) has any deterministic relation to z (*t=0*) and v (*t=0*). What is more: if we can measure z (*t*), and attribute a specific number to it, we have no way of saying with certainty what v (*t*) is. This is what the then-emerging quantum mechanics in the 1920s had to say. The loss of determinism and causality is connected with the fact that the laws of quantum mechanics are chance-based, i.e., probabilistic: we cannot say where the electron is; we can only assign a certain probability of finding the (specific) position of the electron. Thus, the position or velocity of a subatomic particle, like an electron, is *random*.

The above discussion implies that the table, in Tagore's allegorical description, appears static, yet its constituent building blocks (protons, neutrons, electrons, etc.) are in incessant random motion. Hence, a macro-object like a table is described by the classical laws of physics, whereas its building blocks are governed by quantum laws. Thus, there is 'order out of disorder' (randomness). Tagore has mentioned this phenomenon in *Visva Parichay*, where he had written:

> The description is somewhat like this. If we continue to tear a mud house into pieces, we are left with dust. When we cannot further pulverise the dust we feel we have reached to the basic constituent of the mud house. Similarly, physicists thought that when the worldly objects are reduced to a stage when they cannot be further subdivided we reach the atomic world. Atoms are so minute that ten crores of atoms make a line of one inch! We cannot of course break dust by simple means, but physicists have found ways of even breaking open the seemingly impregnable doors of atoms. When the latter are ripped apart we obtain sub-atoms—namely electrons and protons. In order to give an idea of the size we are talking about, a renowned Astronomer has said, 'the space within the atom in which the electrons move about is like an emptied Howrah station in which five or six wasps are let loose.' But, what constrains these electrons within the vast empty space of atoms is the mass concentrated at the atomic centre that is the nucleus. Otherwise the atoms would not have existed, neither would the world we live in…

It should be mentioned at the outset that the randomness, alluded to above, is intrinsic to quantum mechanics and has nothing to do with another kind of randomness that ensues (even in classical physics) because of temperature. For a finite-temperature material, composed of an infinitely large number of constituent microscopic particles, a new attribute called 'entropy' comes into play, in addition to energy. That is why such a material is to be described by the laws of thermodynamics, which had already taken roots far before quantum mechanics came into being. This randomness, implied in thermodynamics, has been aptly described by Tagore in *Visva Parichay*:

> …A physical macro object like a lump of stone or iron appears static from outside—as though it is an epitome of motionlessness. However, it has been proven that molecules and atoms which constitute these bodies, are so miniscule that we cannot see them by normal means, but are forever in a state of vibration. They vibrate when they are hot, they also vibrate when they are cold—only the degree of vibration varies. Indeed, more vigorous the vibration is, hotter is the object, as is felt by our senses. As we keep heating iron for instance, the constituent atoms get so unsettled that their excitement cannot be hidden. The vibrations accompanying the excitement that send waves through our nerves are what is referred to as heat wave. Indeed, heat hits us—light hits eyes, heat hits our body…

We now paraphrase the Einstein-Tagore conversation that took place at the residence of a common friend Mendel in Caputh, a suburb of Berlin:

> Tagore: I was discussing with Dr Mendel today the new mathematical discoveries which tell us that in the realm of infinitesimal atoms chance has its play; the drama of existence is not absolutely predestined in character.
>
> Einstein: The facts that make science tend toward this view do not say goodbye to causality…One tries to understand how the order is in the higher plane. The order is there, where the big elements combine and guide existence, but in the minute elements this order is not perceptible.
>
> Tagore: Thus duality is in the depths of existence, the contradiction of 'free impulse' and the 'directive will' which

works upon it, to evolve an orderly scheme of things.

Einstein: Modern physics would not say they are contradictory. Clouds look as one from a distance, but if you see them nearby, they show themselves as disorderly drops of water.

Tagore: I find a parallel in human psychology. Our passions and desires are unruly, but our character subdues these elements into a harmonious whole. Does something similar to this happen in the physical world? Are the elements rebellious, dynamic with individual impulse? And is there a principle in the physical world which dominates them and puts them into an orderly organisation?

Einstein: Even the elements are not without statistical order; elements of radium will always maintain their specific order, now and ever onward, just as they have done all along. There is, then, a statistical order in the elements.

Tagore: Otherwise, the drama of existence would be too desultory. It is the constant harmony of chance and determination which makes it eternally new and living.

Einstein: I believe that whatever we do or live for has its causality; it is good, however, that we cannot see through to it.

It is evident from the above dialogue that Tagore was quite comfortable with the notion of randomness and the concomitant absence of determinism, associated with microscopic dynamics in tandem with the orderly behaviour of macro objects. Einstein, on the other hand, was not at ease with the statistical (read: probabilistic) nature of quantum laws.

However, it is not clear if Tagore made any distinction between randomness that exists in quantum description down to zero temperature, or the randomness that occurs because of temperature-induced 'fluctuations' that figure in thermodynamic descriptions of material objects. As I have stressed earlier, Rabindranath had a deep intuitive appreciation of the nature of reality, causality, etc. He did not, however, have the rigorous training of a physicist to fully master the subtle nuances of different kinds of randomness that exist in quantum mechanics or finite-temperature statistical mechanics (thermodynamics), or, for that matter, in the recently developed theory of chaos that characterises the dynamics of *nonlinearly* coupled motions. Tagore's ideas of lack-of-definiteness seem, on the other hand, in tune with the Eastern philosophical basis of how the human mind works.

Einstein, on the other hand, was steadfastly in favour of the view that there is a 'profound order in nature, out there', totally independent of human perception. This is borne out by the animated debate between him and the Nobel Laureate Danish physicist, Neils Bohr, who is credited to have founded the Copenhagen School of Quantum Mechanics. Bohr's stand—not quite identical to Tagore's—was that natural phenomena have meaning only through measurement processes. Tagore's position appears more complex as it is based on mind and consciousness. This position, though in conformity with the modern 'many worlds' interpretation of Quantum Theory, is considered extravagant by many modern physicists. Einstein, too, was a bit taken aback by Tagore's doggedness. This can be discerned by his somewhat mischievous reference to 'Rabi' as 'Rabbi'. Many distinguished physicists, however, have found great depth in Tagore's line of thinking. For example, Brian Josephson, who received the Nobel Prize in physics when he was in his twenties, had commented: 'Tagore is, I think, saying that truth is a subtler concept than Einstein realises.' Ilya Prigogine, the Belgian Nobel laureate in Chemistry (1984) had said: 'Curiously enough, the present evolution of science is running in the direction stated by the great Indian poet.' (*Prigogine and Stengers*, 1984, p.293). This particular remark, I guess, is inspired by Prigogine's belief (belied so far) that Chaos Theory would vindicate the foundation of statistical mechanics/thermodynamics—the subjects that describe ordered states arising out of disorder. Tagore was a protagonist of the underlying philosophy of 'ordered structures emerging from underlying disorder', as his conversation with Einstein on music amplifies.

The Poet's cosmic thoughts, as we know, were embedded in his music. His discourse with Einstein on the issues of reality, mind and perception, observation, and human bonding with the Creator, have all found expressions through numerous songs. Some examples are:

Tai tomaar aanondo aamar 'por
Tumi taai eshechho neeche
Aaamaai noyile, tribhuboneshhor
Tomaar prem hoto je michhe
(Your happiness follows mine
And that is why Thee have descended down.
Without me, O Lord,
Your love would have been meaningless)

Aamar bela je jaai
Shaanj belaate tomaar shure shure shur melaate
(My days turn into evenings,
in my efforts to harmonise with thy tune)

Aamaar hiyaar maajhe lukiye chhile,
dekhte aami paini tomaai dekhte aami paaini…
(I have not been able to locate you as thee have been hidden in
my soul)

Ammar milon laagi tumi ashchho kobe theke
tomar chandra-suryo tomai
rakche kothay dheke
koto kaler sakal–sanjhe
tomar charan-dhani baaje . . .
(From time immemorial Thee have been coming to unite with me,
Your own creation: The Sun and the Moon have not been able
to hide you from me.
Your footsteps have been heard through ages of mornings
and evenings,
Your emissary had brought me Thy message)

It is in this context—and in relation to multiple choices of paths that an electron has to traverse, for instance in the double-slit experiment on diffraction—that Gurudev transited to music when, as has been quoted earlier, he told Einstein:

> Tagore: There is in human affairs an element of elasticity also, some freedom within a small range which is for the expression of our personality. It is like the musical system in India, which is not so rigidly fixed as western music. Our composers give a certain definite outline, a system of melody and rhythmic arrangement, and within a certain limit the player can improvise upon it. He must be one with the law of that particular melody, and then he can give spontaneous expression to his musical feeling within the prescribed regulation. We praise the composer for his genius in creating a foundation along with a superstructure of melodies, but we expect from the player his own skill in the creation of variations of melodic flourish and ornamentation. In creation we follow the central law of existence, but if we do not cut ourselves adrift from it, we can have sufficient freedom within the limits of our personality for the fullest self-expression.
>
> Einstein: That is possible only when there is a strong artistic tradition in music to guide the people's mind. In Europe, music has come too far away from popular art and popular feeling and has become something like a secret art with conventions and traditions of its own.
>
> Tagore: You have to be absolutely obedient to this too complicated music. In India, the measure of a singer's freedom is in his own creative personality. He can sing the composer's song as his own, if he has the power of creativity to assert himself in his interpretation of the general law of the melody which he is given to interpret.
>
> Einstein: It requires a very high standard of art to realise fully the great idea in the original music, so that one can make variations upon it. In our country, the variations are often prescribed.

Tagore: If in our conduct we can follow the law of goodness, we can have real liberty of self-expression. The principle of conduct is there, but the character which makes it true and individual is our own creation. In our music there is a duality of freedom and prescribed order.

Einstein: Are the words of a song also free? I mean to say, is the singer at liberty to add his own words to the song which he is singing?

Tagore: Yes. In Bengal we have a kind of song—we call it 'kirtan'—which gives freedom to the singer to introduce parenthetical comments, phrases not in the original song. This occasions great enthusiasm, since the audience is constantly thrilled by some beautiful, spontaneous sentiment added by the singer.

Einstein: Is the metrical form quite severe?

Tagore: Yes, quite. You cannot exceed the limits of versification; the singer in all his variations must keep the rhythm and the time, which is fixed. In European music you have a comparative liberty with time, but not with melody.

Einstein: Can the Indian music be sung without words? Can one understand a song without words?

Tagore: Yes, we have songs with unmeaning words, sounds which just help to act as carriers of the notes. In North India, music is an independent art, not the interpretation of words and thoughts, as in Bengal. The music is very intricate and subtle and is a complete world of melody by itself.

Einstein: Is it not polyphonic?

Tagore: Instruments are used, not for harmony, but for keeping time and adding to the volume and depth. Has melody suffered in your music by the imposition of harmony?

Einstein: Sometimes it does suffer very much. Sometimes the harmony swallows up the melody altogether.

Tagore: Melody and harmony are like lines and colours in pictures. A simple linear picture may be completely beautiful;

the introduction of color may make it vague and insignificant. Yet colour may, by combination with lines, create great pictures, so long as it does not smother and destroy their value.

Einstein: It is a beautiful comparison; line is also much older than colour. It seems that your melody is much richer in structure than ours. Japanese music also seems to be so.

Tagore: It is difficult to analyse the effect of eastern and western music on our minds. I am deeply moved by the western music; I feel that it is great, that it is vast in its structure and grand in its composition. Our own music touches me more deeply by its fundamental lyrical appeal. European music is epic in character; it has a broad background and is Gothic in its structure.

Einstein: This is a question we Europeans cannot properly answer, we are so used to our own music. We want to know whether our own music is a conventional or a fundamental human feeling, whether to feel consonance and dissonance is natural, or a convention which we accept.

Tagore: Somehow the piano confounds me. The violin pleases me much more.

Einstein: It would be interesting to study the effects of European music on an Indian who had never heard it when he was young.

Tagore: Once I asked an English musician to analyse for me some classical music, and explain to me what elements make for the beauty of the piece.

Einstein: The difficulty is that the really good music, whether of the East or of the West, cannot be analysed.

Tagore: Yes, and what deeply affects the hearer is beyond himself.

Einstein: The same uncertainty will always be there about everything fundamental in our experience, in our reaction to art, whether in Europe or in Asia. Even the red flower I see before me on your table may not be the same to you and me.

Tagore: And yet there is always going on the process of

> reconciliation between them, the individual taste conforming to the universal standard.

Note that, at the end of the conversation on music, Einstein himself raises the question of uncertainty about everything fundamental in our experience, while Tagore signs off by highlighting the process of reconciliation in reaching a universal standard, individual taste notwithstanding. This philosophical thought, though metaphorically couched in the discussion on music, is also rooted in the probabilistic interpretation of quantum mechanics that led to the uncertainty of simultaneous measurement of two physical attributes, such as the position and velocity of a quantum particle.

It is clear that the Einstein-Tagore dialogue throws up very complex issues that plague philosophers and scientists alike. In 1611, Galileo had

Einstein with Rabindranath Tagore

said: 'It would seem ridiculous to me to believe that things in nature begin to exist when we begin to discover and understand them'. This is a position diametrically opposite to Tagore's. Perhaps, for now, we remain befuddled with the lingering thought, succinctly expressed by the last century's most eloquent and creative physicist, the Nobel Laureate Richard P. Feynman, who shortly before his death, pronounced:

> The problem of existence is a very interesting and difficult one…When you discover things in mathematics you get the idea that somehow they existed somewhere, but there's nowhere for such things…Well, in the case of Physics we have double trouble. We come upon these mathematical interrelationships but they apply to the universe, so the problem of where they are is doubly confusing…Those are philosophical questions that I don't know how to answer.

a universalist who transcended geographical boundaries and time-zones and left an indelible mark as a thinker above all. These thoughts form the very foundation of Visva-Bharati.

The event of Tagore's birth in Jorasanko, Kolkata, in my parlance of statistical physics is but a 'fluctuation'—a random, chance phenomenon—a process in which Tagore himself evinced keen interest, as described in the last chapter on his discourse with Albert Einstein on Quantum Theory.

Tagore was born in the British capital of India—then Calcutta, in a well-to-do, emancipated and culturally rich family. His grandfather, Prince Dwarkanath, was a shipping magnate who was able to successfully carry out his business in spite of the omnipresence of the imperial regime. His elder brother Satyendranath was the first native entrant in the Indian Civil Service, sometimes facetiously referred to as the Imperial Civil Service. Thus the civil society component of the Raj, rooted in democratic values, had already rubbed on Tagore's upbringing. Coupled with that was the dominating spiritual influence of his father Maharshi Debendranath, who was deeply influenced by Upanishadic thoughts and Sufism. This remarkable confluence and synergy naturally shaped the Tagorean model of education.

Tagore belonged to the Renaissance period of Bengal, which saw the birth of some extraordinary individuals within a span of five to six years—Jagadish Chandra Bose (1858), Rabindranath (1861), Acharya Prafulla Chandra Ray (1861), and Sir Ashutosh Mukherjee (1864). Like Tagore they were all institution builders and exploring their remarkable friendship was another great influence on me.

The 'universal' Tagore' naturally had numerous encounters with world luminaries such as Albert Einstein, Romain Rolland, Jawaharlal Nehru, Sigmund Freud, Victoria Ocampo, to name a few. Einstein, Nehru and Ocampo figure prominently in this book. So does Sarat Chandra Bose, the elder brother of Subhas Chandra who, like Tagore, was torn between the necessity of seeing an emergent Indian nationhood and the same time, the pain of witnessing the plight of Bengal, which eventually suffered the ignominy and trauma of partition.

Conclusion

A Random Walk in Santiniketan Ashram is not a memoir. It is, rather, a collection of essays that I penned from 2012–2014, on different occasions, in my capacity as Vice Chancellor, Visva-Bharati.

In this book, I have made an attempt as a serving Vice Chancellor to present the readers the visionary concepts of Tagore and his creation: Visva-Bharati. The latter is not a standard university but a unique one that subsumes two kindergartens and two high schools in addition to university departments in all areas of arts and sciences, in order to provide an integrated and holistic form of education, in which music and fine arts constitute a critical component. Tagore's concerns for the community and the environment are reflected in the significant programmes of rural reconstruction and village crafts.

As iterated in the Preface, my experience in Visva-Bharati came as the culmination after a forty-year long career in India as a teacher and researcher in physics, as a scientist-cum-academic administrator, as an institution builder and more importantly as an educationist. More than anything, it was an opportunity to rediscover myself in the overall presence of the remarkable personality of Tagore. Like the solar system in which the sun is at the centre of gravity, my intellectual space in Santiniketan was naturally centered on 'Robi' or Rabindranath. He is an epitome of

A Random Walk in Sanitiniketan Ashram is, indeed, a random foray into my Visva-Bharati exposure. Evidently, there ought to be a disclaimer—my thoughts do not lend to an exhaustive survey of Tagore's thoughts or ideals, or his creativity. My 'walk' terminates in a maze of questions. Even though I believe that the Tagore model of education is relevant, I have aired my apprehension regarding Visva Bharati. The Visva-Bharati system seems to have become 'thermodynamically unstable' due to rampant provincialism, in-breeding and political interference—something which Tagore abhorred. Changing Visva-Bharati into a full-fledged university, shackled by rules, regulations and governmental decrees, appears to have been a mistake as rightly feared by our far-sighted parliamentarians when the central university bill was being presented by the-then education minister Maulana Abul Kalam Azad. Today's Visva-Bharati may have ceased to be an Ashram but the magnificent influence of Gurudev Rabindranath lives on in Santiniketan and much beyond.